A Field
Guide to

ROADSIDE
TECHNOLOGY

ED SOBEY

CHICAGO
REVIEW
PRESS

Library of Congress Cataloging-in-Publication Data

Sobey, Edwin J. C., 1948–
    A field guide to roadside technology / Ed Sobey.— 1st ed.
    p. cm.
    Includes bibliographical references and index.
    ISBN 1-55652-609-1
    1. Roads—Accessories. 2. Traffic signs and signals.
3. Electronic apparatus and appliances. I. Title.

TE228.S63 2006
625.7'9—dc22

                              2006002979

Cover and interior design: Joan Sommers

Photo credits: page 50, © 2006 American Consulting Engineers, PLC; page 30, Astro Products; page 112, Automatic Lightning Protection; page 31, City of Lacey; page 155, Jan Fardell; page 173, L. Clark Ford, Birdtex; page 84, International Boundary Commission; page 138, Paul Hellenberg; page 50, Jacobs Engineering Group; page 36, Paul H. Krueger, Florida Turnpike Enterprise; page 32, Greg Leege; page 133, Lincoln Laboratory; page 45, David Denenberg; page 96, Jim Maloney; page 48, Art Mayoff; pages 42 and 43, Multnomah County, Oregon; page 129, National Radio Astronomy Observatory; page 99, National Renewable Energy Laboratory; page 140, National Weather Service; page 61, Orchard Rite Ltd., Inc.; page 160, Oregon State University/ Pete Zerr; pages 89, 91, 92, 93, 97, and 105, Guy Pipitone; pages 4, 14, 21, 22, 28, 38, 47, 51, 59, 60, 62, 64, 71, 72, 80, 88, 95, 102, 107, 114, 115, 117, 118, 122, 128, 130, 136, 148, 149, 164, 169, 172, 174, 179, 186, 189, Rich Sidwa; pages 13, 16, 18, 19, 20, 23, 25, 26, 27, 33, 34, 35, 40, 41, 44, 46, 52, 54, 55, 57, 58, 63, 65, 66, 68, 69, 70, 73, 74, 75, 76, 77, 78, 79, 81, 82, 85, 86, 100, 104, 108, 110, 113, 116, 121, 124, 125, 126, 134, 135, 137, 141, 142, 143, 144, 146, 147, 150, 151, 152, 153, 154, 157, 158, 159, 162, 165, 166, 167, 168, 170, 176, 177, 178, 182, 183, 184, 185, 187, 188, 190, 192, 193, 194, 195, 196, 197, 198, 199, Ed Sobey; page 83, Dave Steele; page 29, Ed Trigg; page 94, photo courtesy of TXU Generation Company LP, Dallas, Texas; page 161, USGS; page 156, Marie Wise; page 106, Xcel Energy Corporation. All rights reserved.

To Jean and John,
whose curiosity and thirst for adventure have taken them around the world and back home to Oregon.

CONTENTS

ACKNOWLEDGMENTS

WRITING THIS BOOK GAVE ME the opportunity to meet dozens of interesting people and to learn how stuff works. I enjoyed learning from the experts and I thank them all.

Glenn Kuhn graciously answered my questions about cellular telephone service and antennas, and he reviewed that part of the text. Thanks, Glenn.

John Weigant, nautical authority, helped me with aids to navigation. He even let me steer his sailboat. That's trust.

Marie Wise, who is with the Port of Longview, Washington, enthusiastically provided photographs of ships and port operations. She took the photograph of the *Ocean Rainbow* and sent the photograph of the *Rubin Kobe* log carrier, which was taken by Jan Fardell.

Ed Trigg, inventor and entrepreneur, provided photographs of and information on his microwave overheight vehicle detector.

Nelson Monroe, Water Operations Supervisor for the City of Redmond, Washington, guided me through his city's water system and toured me through pump stations, tanks, and wells. Wastewater is a different department, and for that I turned to Denise Chanez with the Wastewater Treatment Division of King County, Washington. Vern Allemand, Wastewater Crew Chief for the City of Snoqualmie, Washington, gave me a tour of that city's new treatment plant and explained its operation.

Jim Deal of Crowley Marine arranged for me to join the *Chief*, one of the company's tugboats, so I could get photographs of ships and marine terminals in Seattle. Richard Schwab of Verizon guided me through the maze of wires that make up the telephone system, from central office to home.

Woody Ross, a retired Puget Sound Energy lineman, led me from the Snoqualmie Falls hydroelectric facility to the home wall outlet, explaining how the electrical distribution system works. My friend from Ohio, Guy Pipitone, provided photographs and explanations of electrical generating plants. Jim Maloney, with the Eugene Water & Electric Board in Eugene, Oregon, steered me to information on wind generation of electricity. William Skaff offered advice on differentiating nuclear power plants from fossil fuel plants.

One of my running routes takes me past a fish wheel on Bear Creek. Taking my camera one day to get a photograph of the wheel, I happened to meet fisheries biologist Lindsey Fleischer. She showed me how the wheel works and how salmon are tagged. Luis A. Fuste, Information Officer with the U. S. Geological Service (USGS), provided information on stream gauging stations.

Several people contributed photographs. The beautiful shot of the Golden Gate Bridge came from Art Mayoff. Automatic Lightning Protection provided the photograph of lightning rods. Carol DiQuilio of Reef Industries sent me the photograph of the aerial survey marker.

Randy Stegemeyer of Port Orchard, Washington, provided information on antennas in general and on radio telescope antennas in particular. He also provided a photograph of his radio telescope.

Greg Leege with the Washington State Department of Transportation provided the photograph of the highway advisory radio and explained to me how it worked. Matthew Van Valkenburgh, Director of the Fresno Yosemite International Airport, helped me get photographs from the airport and answered my questions.

Several friends who run with me contributed in several places. Steve McCracken helped me unravel some of the mysteries of the telephone system. Mary Ann Olson and Ryan Olson gave me additional guidance on traffic devices and vehicles.

Keith Berisford of ATT Broadband took me on a tour of a cable system in Redmond, Washington, and Kirkland, Washington, and answered my many questions—thanks, Keith. A chance encounter along the road resulted in my gaining additional clarification about the cable system thanks to Sean Collins.

Mike Whiteaker of the Bellevue, Washington, Traffic Engineering Department guided me through the labyrinth of information regarding traffic signals. Candy Masters helped me with traffic counters. Mike and Candy's boss, Dirk Mitchell, was kind enough to let them spend time with me.

Pat Culbert, Director of Media Relations for Xcel Energy, provided photographs of cooling towers. Rose M. Sabijon and Tanya Cooper of the National Petrochemical & Refiners Association provided the photograph of the refinery. Derek Locke provided the photograph of the cow standing on the cantilever bridge. Nice shot, Derek.

Jordan Thompson provided me great help in figuring out the wireless Internet.

First Calls Uplink provided me with the photograph of its uplink truck. Bill Evans of TowerKill.com told me about the effectiveness of bird deflectors.

Peggy Laramie, American Gas Association Director of Public Relations, gave me information on gas transportation systems. Jodi Wright and Cathy Reynolds of Pacific Northwest Natural Gas identified the gas regulator that I photographed on the outskirts of Astoria, Oregon. Thank you, ladies.

Albert Alvareztorres Jr., with the American Radio Relay League, identified the ham radio antenna found in the photo in this book and provided information about it.

Dave Steele, Washington State Surveyor, provided great photographs of survey markers and border monuments, and he wrote up a summary of monuments for me. Dean Dan Bartell at California State

University, Fresno, helped me identify irrigation systems in photographs. Professor Bill Dornfeld reviewed the manuscript and offered helpful suggestions for improving it.

Many of the photographs were taken by Rich Sidwa, and I am deeply thankful for his help.

Obviously, many people contributed to the writing of this book. I extend a hearty thank you to each of you.

INTRODUCTION

AS YOU WALK AROUND your neighborhood you see machines that work for you, but you may not know what they do. However, if one of them breaks or has to be replaced, you certainly notice the interruption in service. Your water may be shut off for a few hours. You might lose phone service, electrical power, or the cable signal for your television. When "that thing" on the utility pole or on the ground breaks, you realize how important it is to you. *A Field Guide to Roadside Technology* will help you figure out what "that thing" is and how it works. Some field guides help you identify birds or trees you see. This book identifies devices made by people.

A Field Guide to Roadside Technology will help you be a technology detective. You can find out which of your neighbors has cable television. You can figure out what the tangle of wires is on a utility pole, or what a particular antenna is for. You can look at a ship and quickly figure out what type it is and what functions it performs.

You can use this book in several ways. Of course, you can start on the first page and read through to the end. However, my intention is that you will keep this book handy as you travel, so that whenever you see some gizmo that you don't recognize, you can look it up to find out what it is and what it does.

To find out about that odd machine you see, refer first to the Contents. Devices are grouped by type (Bridges or Antennas, for example) or the locations in which they are found. Within each chapter, similar devices or devices that are part of a long system are grouped together. For example, you can follow the path of your home telephone system from a utility pole all the way to your house by reading successive entries. Start with the chapter that best corresponds to where you see an object you want to look up. For example, if you're near an airport, go to chapter 7, "In the Air and Near Airports." Or if you're looking at something that's attached to a utility pole, go to chapter 9, "On Utility Poles and Towers." Thumb through the pages and look at the pictures and the written descriptions of objects to figure out what it is you're looking at. You may have to look in a couple of chapters to find what you see. Although most of the telephone and cable systems are included in chapter 9, for example, related devices that sit on the ground are included in chapter 4, "On the Ground." You can also look in the Index, where you'll find entries grouped by subject.

A THOUGHT ON SAFETY

Of course, I want you to explore safely and responsibly. Don't open covers, pull on wires or pipes, or try to take things apart. Although the machines around you were put there to serve you, some of them can hurt you. So explore at a safe distance, with your hands buried in your pockets. Be safe while learning and having fun.

Although this book contains information on many of the most commonly seen or used devices, it would be impossible for any book to cover every single gizmo out there in the world. There are hundreds of devices that play roles in our lives. If you find one that's not in the book but, in your opinion, should be, please let me know. Maybe it'll be it in a future edition. Contact me through my publisher at:

Ed Sobey, author of *A Field Guide to Roadside Technology*
c/o Chicago Review Press
814 N. Franklin Street
Chicago, IL 60610

While it's certainly important to know what things are, it's far more important to exercise your inquiring mind. Look for more roadside technology and ask questions. Your questions may encourage others to think about the technical environment we live in, and maybe they'll ask questions, too. These questions lead to learning and understanding.

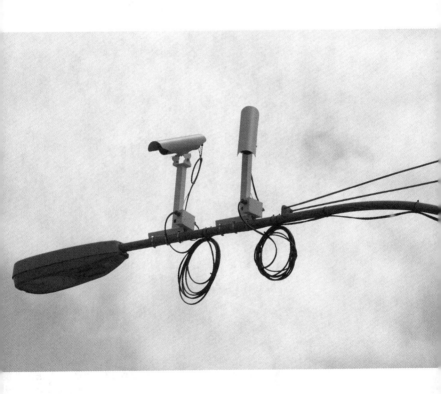

HIGHWAYS AND ROADWAYS

HIGHWAYS AND ROADWAYS ARE technology showcases zipping past your car window as you travel along at 60 MPH (100 KM/H). Every few seconds you whiz by yet another piece of machinery. Luckily, the same type of device is often found at every intersection or every few miles, so you have many opportunities to see and identify each one.

Since state and local governments maintain their own roads and highways, many of the devices you see aren't uniform across the country. Highway devices in California may not look exactly like similar devices in Massachusetts. However, if you can identify a machine in one location, you will have clues as to what a device of similar size and shape does in a different location, even if it isn't exactly the same.

Traffic Signal

BEHAVIOR
Controls traffic by indicating which lane of cars should move through the intersection.

HABITAT
At busy intersections.

HOW IT WORKS

Watch a traffic signal and you'll figure out that it uses a timer. The light stays green for maybe 30 seconds, turns yellow for 5 or so seconds, then turns red for perhaps 35 seconds while the green and yellow lights for the other lanes of traffic complete their cycles.

Traffic engineers set the times for each part of the cycle based on the traffic load on each street. They may also change the cycle to run faster at night when there are fewer cars on the road. Many traffic signals are also controlled by switches (see below).

UNIQUE CHARACTERISTICS

Does the red light look different from the yellow and green lights? Instead of using normal incandescent light bulbs (like the ones you use at home) for red lights, many cities now use LEDs, or light-emitting diodes. LEDs have a deeper color than incandescent bulbs. You can see the many sources of light, which are the individual diodes. It takes dozens of tiny LEDs to make up one red traffic light.

LEDs are much more expensive than regular lights. Why would traffic departments switch to a more expensive light? LEDs can last as long as 10 years—several times longer than traditional lights. The expense of sending a crew out to change a traffic light bulb is so great that it's cheaper to use a more expensive light source that lasts longer. Lighting engineers just recently developed good yellow and green LEDs, and traffic departments are starting to install those colors now.

If you see a traffic signal that uses incandescent bulbs open for repair, look inside to see what color the bulbs are. They might not be red, green, and yellow. Some cities use a yellow bulb shining through a blue cover to make a green light.

Increasingly, engineers are installing additional devices called switches to control the lights as well. At an intersection, look for dark lines in the shape of a square or rectangle in the road's surface. The dark lines are patched strips in the road where workers sawed up the original roadway to install an *induction vehicle detector* (see page 19), which consists of loops, or coils, of wire that detect cars and change traffic lights accordingly.

At some intersections you'll see other devices that prompt traffic lights to change. These include *video detection cameras* (see page 20) and *microwave vehicle detectors* (see page 20), which are mounted on traffic poles.

Old traffic signals use mechanical systems to turn each light on and off. You can hear the motors and switches inside these signals working as the lights change.

Modern traffic signals use electronic circuits instead of mechanical systems to control the lights. The next time you're stopped at one of these, look for the *traffic signal control box* (see page 18), which houses the signal's timer, or clock, and switches. It may be mounted on one of the traffic-signal poles or placed on the ground behind the signal.

INTERESTING FACTS

Traffic lights were used even before automobiles were invented. Starting in 1868, the British used red and green lights to control horse carriage traffic at busy intersections. A police officer had to manually switch the lights from red to green and back. The use of a yellow light also originated in Great Britain, in 1918.

The first red and green traffic lights in America appeared in Cleveland, Ohio, in 1914. A police officer, William Potts, created the first three-color light used in the United States and had it installed in Detroit in 1920. Three years later the famous inventor Garrett Augustus Morgan invented the automatic traffic light.

Traffic Signal Control Box

BEHAVIOR
Houses electronic circuits and power supplies that control traffic lights.

HABITAT
At any intersection where you find a modern traffic signal you will find one or two control boxes, usually on one of the corners of the intersection. Often, as is the case shown here, you will see two boxes. One houses the electronic circuits and the other houses power supplies for the traffic signal.

HOW IT WORKS
One box (shown on the left in this photo) controls the signals. Inside it is a computer. The computer can be set to change the traffic lights at set time periods. For example, it may be set to cycle through the green, yellow, and red lights every 30 seconds. The timing can be set to change throughout the day to accommodate changes in traffic patterns. Traffic engineers study the flow of traffic and program a computer to run the lights accordingly.

If there is an *induction vehicle detector* (see page 19) at the intersection, its signals go into the control computer as well. As a car pulls up to the intersection and stops above the detector's wire ground loop, the sensor (loop) sends a message to the computer, which prompts the traffic light to change.

The second box distributes power to the computer and the traffic signal. Electrical power comes into this box from electric wires located on utility poles or underground. Inside this box are the connections.

What color is the green light? Most incandescent light bulbs used in traffic signals emit white light. To get the red, yellow, and green colors you see, the light from the bulbs shines through colored glass covers. You might detect a bluish tint to green lights. Blue is incorporated in the green light's cover to help people who are red-green colorblind see a difference between the stop and go lights.

Induction Vehicle Detector

BEHAVIOR
When a vehicle moves over the detector, the detector sends a message to the traffic signal's computer to start the cycle to change the lights.

HABITAT
Busy intersections. Look on the ground for a thin bead of black asphalt that covers up the square or rectangle of wire that was installed after the road was last paved.

HOW IT WORKS
This operates in the same way as do the metal detectors you see people using at the beach or in a park. An electric current flows through the coil of wires under the street. As a car moves over the coil, the car's metal changes the magnetic field in the coil. A sensor in the circuit of the coil detects the change in the magnetic field and sends a signal to the computer in the control box.

UNIQUE CHARACTERISTICS
Some cities mark the place in the road that covers the most sensitive area of the coil with an "X" so people riding bicycles know where to stop. Since bikes have much less metal than cars, the detector might not notice the change in the magnetic field caused by the bike unless it is placed directly over the most sensitive area of the coil. The mark shows where the bicyclists should stop to change the signal.

INTERESTING FACTS
The wire coils are set about two inches below the top of the road's surface. Workers use a rotary saw to cut grooves in the road. Then they place the wire in the grooves and seal the wires into the road with hot asphalt, which is the dark line you see.

Video Detection Camera

BEHAVIOR

Detects cars stopped at an intersection and sends a message to the traffic signal's computer to begin the cycle of light changes.

This camera takes the place of an *induction vehicle detector* (see page 19), which uses magnetic loops buried in the road. The advantages of a video detection camera over an induction vehicle detector are twofold: engineers can set the camera in place quickly, and they do not have to disrupt traffic by digging up the road to install loops.

HABITAT

At intersections, directly above the arm that supports a traffic signal. You can distinguish it from a *traffic surveillance camera* (see page 23) in two ways. First, it is mounted on a shorter arm or pole than is a surveillance camera. Second, it is fixed in place—it has no motor to move it, so it can't pan (turn sideways) or tilt (move up and down).

HOW IT WORKS

A computer monitors certain points within the image picked up by the camera's field of view. When most or all of those points change (because a car comes into the view), the computer sends a message to the traffic signal's computer to change the light.

INTERESTING FACTS

Optical sensing technology is improving quickly; look for this device to replace the induction vehicle detector in the near future.

Microwave Vehicle Detector

BEHAVIOR

Uses microwaves (radar) to detect vehicles at an intersection so it can trigger the traffic signal's computer to change the lights.

HABITAT

Permanent installations and temporary installations where induction vehicle detectors have been dug up. Most often these are dug up to repair the road surface. It is mounted on a signal arm (a pipe that supports a traffic signal over the road).

HOW IT WORKS

The microwave vehicle detector sends out a radar beam. When the beam bounces off a car the reflected signal is detected and trips a switch in the detector, which sends a message to the traffic signal's computer to change the light.

UNIQUE CHARACTERISTICS

The detector is about six inches (15 cm) long and four inches (10 cm) high. The front is covered with black film that keeps out light (and dirt) while allowing microwaves to pass through.

Emergency Preemption Detector

BEHAVIOR
Controls traffic signals so emergency vehicles can get through intersections faster.

HABITAT
Located above the lanes of traffic, on top of the support arms that hold up traffic lights.

HOW IT WORKS
Emergency vehicles have flashing (strobe) lights that activate the detector. The lights may be either visible or infrared. Infrared light has wavelengths too long for human eyes to see.

Typically a detector is set to respond to strobe lights when they first appear about 1,000 feet (300 m) from the intersection. This gives time for the signal light to change and for cars ahead of the emergency vehicle to move through the intersection and out of the way.

Some cities' emergency preemption detectors have two levels of operation. One level, High Priority, is for emergency vehicles; the other, Low Priority, is for buses.

UNIQUE CHARACTERISTICS
Look for the distinctive shape on top of traffic light arms. The detector is taller than it is wide, is dark in color, and typically has two shields that project outward, like the bills of two baseball hats, one above the other.

Traffic Surveillance Camera

BEHAVIOR
Videotapes traffic so engineers can improve traffic flow by making changes to signals and signage.

HABITAT
Along major highways and at busy intersections. The camera is mounted on a tall pole or a long arm that extends above a traffic signal. Engineers set the camera up high so it can capture a wide field of vision.

HOW IT WORKS
The video recorded by this type of camera may be no match for *The Simpsons* in terms of entertainment value, but a traffic surveillance camera does capture important information. By examining the recording via monitors, engineers can study the movement of cars and determine how they should change the timing of traffic signals.

Engineers can tilt the camera up and down and pan it left and right to see traffic in all directions. No one sits at the monitors watching traffic all day, so if you make faces at the camera it's likely that no one will see you. But when a problem arises, the engineers can look to see what's happening and can record the scenes on magnetic tape.

In some areas, engineers have turned traffic surveillance cameras into Web cams that allow people to check for traffic backups via the Internet. To see traffic conditions around Seattle, for example, viewers can check the Washington State Department of Transportation's Web site (www.wsdot.wa.gov/traffic/seattle), which offers links to several such Web cams. California's Caltrans Web site (http://video.dot.ca.gov) offers viewers access to live feed from hundreds of cameras monitoring sections of freeways throughout the state, and the New York City Department of Transportation offers traffic-surveillance Web cams at its Advanced Traveler Information System Web site (http://nyctmc.org/). Those interested in seeing what traffic's like in Philadelphia can log onto http://Philadelphia.pahighways.com/expressways. For a comprehensive array of links to traffic-surveillance Web cams in major cities throughout the United States, check out the Where in Federal Contracting? Web site (www.wifcon.com/gettingsummeruscities.htm).

Traffic Counter

BEHAVIOR
Records the number of vehicles using the road via rubber hoses. Traffic engineers use this data to determine if there is too much traffic for the road to handle.

HABITAT
On any road except a high-speed highway.

HOW IT WORKS
Rubber hoses are laid across a road. These are attached to the counter, a device housed in a metal box that is placed alongside the road. As cars, trucks, and even bicycles cross the rubber hoses, they compress the hoses, sending blasts of air into the counter. The air moves a diaphragm that is connected to a switch. The switch then sends an electrical signal to circuits inside the counter that record the traffic count.

Typically a counter has two hoses. One hose stretches across the entire road and the other reaches only the center of the road. The counts from the two hoses are recorded separately. The count for one direction of traffic is taken from the short hose. The count for the other direction of traffic is obtained by subtracting the count produced by the shorter hose from the count produced by the longer hose. Each count is divided by two (because the average vehicle has two axles) to determine the approximate number of vehicles traveling in a particular direction on that road.

INTERESTING FACTS
Engineers also use traffic counters to calculate vehicle speeds. The counters record the length of time that passes between the moment that a vehicle's front tires depress the hose and the moment that its rear tires depress it. Traffic counters aren't used as a way to catch and issue tickets to speeding drivers, but the vehicle-speed information they record is used to determine if there is a need to post speed-limit signs or other signs designed to slow traffic.

Audible Crossing Signal

BEHAVIOR
Allows blind people to cross intersections safely by audibly indicating when they have the green light to cross.

HABITAT
In many cities, at intersections that feature traffic signals for pedestrians as well as vehicles.

HOW IT WORKS
Because it does no good to have just one audible signal that a crossing light is on (the blind can't see in which direction it is safe to cross), there are two audible signals. Chirping sounds indicate that it's safe to cross streets in the east-west directions and coo-coo sounds indicate that it's safe to cross in the north-south directions. This system requires the blind to have a mental map of the streets, to know where they are and where they are going, and to have a good sense of direction.

INTERESTING FACTS
A new device is being installed to help people who are both deaf and blind so they can safely cross intersections. This device displays a tactile signal that a person can identify when he or she touches the crosswalk button.

Parking Meter

BEHAVIOR
Legally allows a driver to park in a specific spot for a period of time in exchange for money.

HABITAT
Along the curbs of streets in commercial sections of towns and cities.

HOW IT WORKS
The old-fashioned type of meter has a spring-driven clock that counts down the minutes left until you get a parking ticket. Ingenious lever mechanisms inside the meter sort coins and monitor the time paid for and used. The newer type of meter uses electronics rather than strictly mechanical systems. In an effort to reduce costs (and to the dismay of parking meter attendants), many cities are doing away with parking meters and are instead using centralized pay stations at curbs and in parking lots.

INTERESTING FACTS
You know what it is, but did you know why it's there? Carl Magee, a newspaper editor and member of the transportation committee of the Oklahoma City Chamber of Commerce, first proposed the idea of parking meters in 1935 as a way to encourage people to do their shopping or other business quickly and move their cars out of the limited parking spaces that were available, allowing others a temporary space to park as well. The idea received an enthusiastic response. As a result, Mr. Magee invented the parking meter, and Oklahoma City was the first city to use the device.

In-Ground Pavement Lighting System

BEHAVIOR

Alerts drivers that pedestrians are crossing the street in the middle of the block.

HABITAT

On the street, in the middle of the block, in a commercial area that has heavy pedestrian traffic.

HOW IT WORKS

The lights are either LEDs (light-emitting diodes) or halogen lights. Pedestrians activate them by pressing a crosswalk button. Because these lights are on for only a few seconds each hour of the day, they last many years—up to 10,000 hours—before they need to be replaced.

Overheight Vehicle Detector and Warning System

BEHAVIOR
Uses microwaves or visible light to detect vehicles that are too tall to safely pass under a structure and to warn drivers of an impending clearance problem. Flashing lights are used to warn drivers; sometimes an alarm sound.

HABITAT
On roadways where drivers will soon encounter a bridge or tunnel entrance, near parking structures, and at weigh stations.

HOW IT WORKS
Most detectors send out microwave beams (radar signals) at a height above the ground that only too-tall vehicles meet. When a vehicle that is too tall passes by, it interrupts the beam of microwaves, which triggers alarms farther down the road to alert the driver.

A "double eye" version of the detector is direction discerning—it can figure out in which direction the vehicle is traveling. More advanced systems use a mixture of both infrared and visible red light sources to minimize the interfering effects of stray or ambient light sources.

The detector is often mounted directly behind a sign that announces "Overheight Vehicle Detector." The system's alarm bell or flashing lights is farther down the road. Both the sign and the alarm may be easier to spot than the detector itself.

INTERESTING FACTS
This system, created by Ed Trigg, a retired army officer, made an immediate impact on the number of accidents in one town. In Newport News, Virginia, more than a dozen accidents involving vehicles that were too tall to pass under a particular bridge had occurred each year for many years. During the year following the installation of the system, there were none.

Radar Gun

BEHAVIOR
Measures the speed of cars so police can ticket people who drive faster than the speed limit.

HABITAT
In many cases, where you're not expecting to find it. State police, highway patrol, and local police officers in most states use some type of radar gun.

HOW IT WORKS
The radar gun sends out a series of pulses of very small radio waves or microwaves. The pulses bounce off cars, and the receiver in the radar gun picks up some of the reflected pulses. It measures the *Doppler shift*, or the change in frequency of the radar signal and uses that to calculate the speed of the car.

Radar pulses that bounce off a building or other stationary object come back at the same frequency as they were sent. However, if pulses hit an object that is moving, such as a car on a highway, the radar signal comes back at a different frequency.

Imagine listening to an ambulance siren approaching and then moving away from you. Moving toward you, the sound waves are heard at a higher pitch, or frequency. Moving away, the pitch seems lower. The faster the speed of the ambulance, the more pronounced the frequency shift.

Instead of sound waves, the radar gun uses electromagnetic radio waves. It measures the shift in the frequency caused by a car's motion and converts that to speed.

Watch for police standing beside or sitting inside their cars holding radar guns, aiming them at passing vehicles. When the guns find speeders, the police flag them over.

Laser Speed Gun

BEHAVIOR
Uses infrared laser light to measure the speed of cars.

HABITAT
You might see a laser speed gun anywhere you might see a police radar gun. Increasingly, police are switching from radar guns to laser speed guns.

HOW IT WORKS
Laser speed guns measure the amount of time it takes a pulse of light to reach a car, reflect off it, and return to the light's source. A computer inside the gun captures this information and uses it to calculate the laser gun's distance from the car. The laser gun takes several such samples in a single second, which allows its computer to very accurately calculate how quickly the distance is changing. The change in distance over a period of time is the speed of the car.

Some laser speed guns come equipped with cameras to record the license plate of a speeding car and photograph both the car and driver. Gotcha! They can install these along a highway, record speeders, and send tickets through the mail (done in some places already). Such a system allows police to ticket many more speeders without facing the danger of pulling cars off busy highways.

Highway Advisory Radio (HAR)

BEHAVIOR

Broadcasts radio messages advising motorists of danger, traffic congestion, or construction on the road in real time (as it is occurring).

HABITAT

HAR transmitters are located in areas throughout the United States. Look for road signs telling you that an advisory radio message is available. Tune your AM radio to the frequency shown on the sign, and as you approach the transmitter's antenna you'll pick up the signal.

HOW IT WORKS

The Highway Advisory Radio (HAR) broadcasts on a low frequency of the AM (amplitude modulated) band, often at 530 kHz. Typically HAR transmitters broadcast using 10 watts and have a range of about one mile (1.6 km).

Beside the transmitter's mast, which holds up the antenna, is a control cabinet. Inside it is a radio transmitter, a voice recorder, and a power supply. Much like the way people leave messages on an answering machine, traffic engineers use a phone line to call in to the transmitter and record messages to be broadcast over the radio. The tall mast used for the antenna improves the transmission of the radio signal by getting it above trees and other ground obstacles.

INTERESTING FACTS

You can gauge a HAR's range right from the comfort of your own car. Tune your radio to the frequency indicated on an HAR sign. As soon as you pick up the broadcast, watch your odometer (or set it back to zero and let it run). See how far you have traveled by the time you can no longer pick up the broadcast. This distance is the HAR's range.

Deer Reflector

BEHAVIOR
It doesn't reflect deer, but it does reflect the light from cars' headlights to scare deer.

HABITAT
Rural highways and roads where there are large populations of deer.

HOW IT WORKS
The reflectors are set on posts in a straight line along the edge of a road. As headlights hit one of the reflectors, the light is reflected to the next reflector. A deer near the road sees a line of light from one reflector to another and hesitates to cross the road in front of the car. It doesn't always work, but the system does dramatically reduce the number of deer killed or injured by cars.

> Some estimates put the number of deer killed on U.S. highways at 500,000 per year.

UNIQUE CHARACTERISTICS
You can identify them by their close (a few yards apart) and uniform spacing. A stretch of road might have thousands of them. You can identify them by their appearance, too. Most highway reflectors are flat, but deer reflectors are three-sided.

Exhaust Plume

BEHAVIOR

The white plume of condensation and exhaust is often visible from the tailpipes of cars on cold mornings. After the car has been in motion for a few minutes, the plume disappears.

HOW IT WORKS

The exhaust plume isn't smoke (combustion particles suspended in air); it's water vapor. When an engine is first started it is cold. It takes several minutes for the engine to warm up and for it to warm up the exhaust pipes. During that time water vapor coming from the engine's exhaust condenses into droplets that we often call steam. After a few minutes, as the tailpipe heats up, the water vapor escapes into the air without having condensed. A white exhaust plume of condensed water vapor lets you know that the car producing them was just started.

Electric Heater Plug

BEHAVIOR
Allows for the connection of a car engine heater to a source of electrical power.

HABITAT
In climates where subfreezing temperatures occur throughout winter, people install heaters in their cars to warm up their cars' engines. The electric heater plug hangs down below the car's front bumper—provided the engine is in the front.

HOW IT WORKS
In some systems, the wires attached to the plug connect to a heating element that's wrapped around the outside of the dipstick. Other systems have a heating element that attaches to the outside of the engine block. In both cases, the plug is inserted into a common household electrical outlet to activate the heater.

If a car's engine becomes too cold, the fluids—even antifreeze—in it can freeze. Upon freezing the fluids expand and can crack the engine block, ruining it—and it's an expensive item to replace. Antifreeze can protect a car's engine to temperatures well below freezing, but in Alaska, Canada, and parts of the upper Midwest, temperatures can plummet below -40° F (-40° C), where even antifreeze freezes.

If a little antifreeze is good for a car, is a lot of antifreeze better? This seems weird, but putting too much antifreeze in a car's cooling system will raise the freezing point, making it easier for the fluid to freeze. Manufacturers recommend mixing antifreeze and water in equal amounts for optimal protection.

Look for the "pig tail" plugs hanging down from under the front bumper of cars. Wherever you see them you know you will need a good winter coat.

INTERESTING FACTS
When cars are running they generate enough heat (from the explosive burning of gasoline inside) to keep cooling fluids quite warm. But turned off, engines quickly cool off.

Toll Payment Transponder

BEHAVIOR
Allows drivers to zip through a toll-collecting station without waiting, stopping, or handing over cash. Instead, a computerized system scans a passing car's attached transponder, identifies the car's vehicle identification number, and deducts the toll from the balance in the car owner's account.

HABITAT
Mounted on the inside of the front windshield of vehicles that are driven in one of the several states that now use this radio toll-collecting system.

HOW IT WORKS
A tiny radio inside the transponder (or card, as it is frequently called) broadcasts the unique vehicle identification number assigned to it. Radio receivers around the road pick up the signal and transmit it to a computer. The computer, called a lane controller, integrates the information for each lane of traffic. The lane controller sends the information to a customer service center, where the toll is deducted from the driver's account. Each month drivers receive reports of their accounts so they know if they need to send a payment to increase the amount of money in their account. Some systems feature a device, which can be kept in the car, that shows drivers how much money remains in that car's toll account. If a car that doesn't have a transponder goes through a transponder lane, a video camera records its license number.

INTERESTING FACTS
When traveling on a toll road or bridge, look for signs directing cars to special lanes. The special lanes have names such as E-Z Pass, E-pass,

Express Toll, Fast Lane, Fast Track, and Sun Pass. If you're on a road or bridge that has these lanes, look for the electronic cards (transponders) mounted on the inside of the front windshields of cars in those lanes. Watch to see how long it takes those cars to get through the toll plaza compared to cars that have to stop to pay cash.

Toll payment transponders save toll agencies the cost of paying people to collect tolls; in some places that use this system, you must now pay a premium to pay a toll in cash.

Similar technology now allows people to pay for purchases in a store merely by swiping a tiny radio transmitter past the cash register detector. This system is called RFID, for radio frequency identification. RFID is used in vending machines, at fast food restaurants, at gas stations, and at stores.

The computerized "cash register" scans an RFID wand and identifies the owner's account number. That information, along with information about the purchase (including the cost), is transmitted to a central computer that charges your credit card or debit card for the transaction.

2 BRIDGES

THERE ARE HUNDREDS of different kinds of bridges. Some are fixed, while others move to let ships pass underneath. There are advantages to both types.

Bridges that move are more expensive to maintain since they have huge motors and gears that are needed to move their massive bridge spans. They also require people to open and shut them. However, fixed bridges that are tall enough to allow big ships to pass underneath them can be quite expensive to build. Also, roads often have to be elevated to get the cars up to the bridge. That's not an issue when the river is far below the roads. But in Florida, where the land is flat, building a fixed bridge to cross a navigable waterway requires long ramps to get vehicles up to a bridge deck that is high enough for ships to pass under it.

Moving bridges can move in several different ways. A section of the bridge, usually the center section, can lift up out of the way. This is a *lift* bridge. Or the bridge's roadway can pivot upward at one or both ends, like a door on a hinge or a drawbridge at a castle moat. This is a *bascule* bridge. A *swing* bridge turns, like a lazy Susan spinning around on a table, but does not lift.

Boats or ships signal the bridge operator either by radio or with a designated blast of the ship's horn. For example, one long blast followed by two short blasts might mean to open a particular bridge. The operator checks the bridge to make sure it's safe to open it, then sounds a warning and turns on flashing lights to alert pedestrians and drivers. When the bridge is clear of traffic, the operator lowers safety barriers. Then the operator turns on the motor to move the bridge. The boat or ship passes under the bridge, and the operator moves the bridge back into place so cars can cross it. In some places bridge openings are restricted to certain hours of the day in order to avoid traffic congestion during rush hours.

Fixed bridges have many different designs and are constructed from many different types of materials. Steel or concrete beams are often used to support short bridges, such as bridges over a highway. Really long bridges are usually suspended by steel cables. These are just two examples of the many designs and materials used in fixed bridges.

Bascule Bridge

BEHAVIOR
One or two sections of the road swing up and out of the way so ship traffic can pass underneath.

HABITAT
At river crossings in cities and along the inland waterways of the East Coast, especially in Florida.

HOW IT WORKS
The center section of the bridge is composed of one or two "leaves" that rotate up. The leaves pivot around hinge-like axles called *trunnions*, which are housed on the base of the bridge. Motors raise the leaves when an operator in the bridge control room turns them on.

To assist the motor in lifting the weight of the bridge sections, each of the leaves has a counterweight, which balances the weight of the bridge. The counterweights of some bascule bridges are attached to the ends of the leaves beneath the roadway, making them difficult to spot.

UNIQUE CHARACTERISTICS
Look for large blocks of concrete (the bridge's counterweights) attached to the land sides of the leaves. (Note: not all counterweights are visible from land.) Also, see if you can see where the bridge operator sits. Look for a sign telling boat operators and ship captains how to raise the bridge.

The next time you watch a bascule bridge with two leaves in action, notice how one leaf begins its ascent before the other. When not in operation, the leaves are locked together to prevent them from moving as cars and trucks pass by. After unlocking them, the operator raises one leaf and then the other so they don't collide.

Lift Bridge

BEHAVIOR
Raises the center road section of a bridge without tilting the section.

HABITAT
On railroad bridges and, to a lesser extent, on automobile bridges that pass over rivers.

HOW IT WORKS
The bridge's machinery and an operator's shack are usually located on top of the center span; this allows the operator good visibility. From here the operator opens the bridge when a ship signals that it needs to pass.

Rather than having huge motors lift the entire weight of the bridge section, each end of the span is supported by counterweights that fall as the section is raised.

UNIQUE CHARACTERISTICS
Easy-to-see counterweights (massive pieces of concrete). As the span rises, watch the counterweights fall.

INTERESTING FACTS
It is common for a lift bridge that is used for railroads to be left in the raised position and lowered only when trains are scheduled to pass over it. This allows ships to pass underneath the bridge without requiring an operator to be there at all times. The operator can arrive just before the scheduled arrival of a train.

Swing Bridge

BEHAVIOR
Opens by pivoting on a center point so it can turn out of the way of ship traffic.

HABITAT
This bridge crosses rivers that have relatively flat banks, which don't provide high-enough elevations for a fixed bridge to be built economically. Railroad bridges are often swing bridges; frequently they are closed to ship traffic only when a train is scheduled to cross.

HOW IT WORKS
An electric motor turns a series of gears that move the bridge on a large pivot point. An operator must be present to run the bridge.

Girder (Beam) Bridge

BEHAVIOR
Supports a roadway over a short distance.

HABITAT
On highways, over streams, and at other locations where a bridge is required to span only a short distance.

HOW IT WORKS
The simplest kind of bridge, a girder or beam bridge is less expensive and easier to construct than other types of bridges. A log that is used to cross a stream is an example of a girder or beam bridge. For road bridges, girders are usually constructed of steel or concrete. Long trucks carry the beams to the construction site, where they are lifted into place. Since the beams are built in a factory rather than on site, bridge construction is faster.

The longer a girder is, the stronger it must be to support its own weight. As its strength increases, however, so does its weight. For this reason, beam or girder bridges are impractical for spanning distances of any length.

UNIQUE CHARACTERISTICS
Often girders form the shape of a capital letter "I." These are called I beams. Another girder shape is the box girder. This girder has four walls that form an enclosed box. It is stronger than an I beam and is used in longer bridges.

Cantilever Bridge

BEHAVIOR
Crosses large spans (often rivers or bays) without the benefit of having a center support.

HABITAT
At crossings of up to 1,800 feet (549 m) in length—the extreme limit of engineering to date.

HOW IT WORKS
The bridge extends over the opening from both sides. Each half of the bridge is a cantilever, meaning that it is supported on just one end. The two cantilevers are anchored at their land ends, much like you might put a brick on the end of a ruler that extends over the edge of a table, or like a diving board that extends over a swimming pool. The two cantilevers connect in the center of the bridge.

UNIQUE CHARACTERISTICS
Most cantilever bridges are built with trusses or steel girders. The center section of the bridge features smaller trusses and the outer sections have larger trusses. The outer trusses have to support both themselves and the center section, so they have to be stronger than the center trusses.

INTERESTING FACTS
The longest cantilever bridge crosses the St. Lawrence River in Canada. The bridge spans 1,800 feet (549 m).

Truss Bridge

BEHAVIOR
Supports a roadway or a train track.

HABITAT
Over rivers or ravines.

HOW IT WORKS
Resembling something constructed from a giant Erector Set, a truss bridge has a skeletal structure of, usually, steel girders. Each of the pieces of the bridge carries a portion of the bridge's weight.

UNIQUE CHARACTERISTICS
The trusses, or metal support beams, can rise above the roadbed or support it from below. As you cross a truss bridge, think of how hard it would be to clean and paint all the metal girders. It's for this reason that some truss bridges are made with steel that doesn't require painting. The outside layer of rust stops the rest of the truss from oxidizing.

Truss bridges feature many different truss arrangements. See if you can identify differences in the ways that two truss bridges are constructed.

INTERESTING FACTS
The longest truss bridge in the world crosses the Columbia River at Astoria, Oregon. The truss section is 1,232 feet (375.5 m) long, and the total bridge length (including approaches) is over four miles (6.4 km).

Arch Bridge

BEHAVIOR
Spans moderately long rivers or valleys.

HABITAT
In the United States this bridge is found primarily throughout the eastern seaboard and on the coastal highway of the West Coast.

HOW IT WORKS
A beautiful structure, the modern arch bridge is constructed from stone or concrete (some older arch bridges are made of iron). The sweeping arch carries the weight of the bridge to the land.

Many ancient stone arches remain today. Since a large arch can span a river, there is no need for a center support, which saves work in construction. Not having a center support also protects the bridge from damage by floodwaters.

INTERESTING FACTS
The Romans constructed arch bridges 2,000 years ago.

The oldest bridge made of iron, the Ironbridge in Ironbridge, England, is an arch bridge. The Ironbridge was built in 1779 across the River Severn by local ironmaster Abraham Darby III. His grandfather, Abraham Darby, was the first ironmaster to succeed in smelting iron using coke rather than charcoal. Currently the author's son Woody lives in the tollbooth of the Ironbridge.

If you travel to Sydney, Australia, check out the Sydney Harbour Bridge, a beautiful arch bridge that is adjacent to the Sydney Opera House. Visitors can actually climb up the bridge—not down where the cars go whizzing by, but up on the structure itself, hundreds of feet about the water.

Suspension Bridge

BEHAVIOR
Carries roadways, suspended by cables from very tall towers, over very wide bodies of water.

HABITAT
Wide rivers and bays throughout the world.

HOW IT WORKS
The bridge's roadway is supported by a series of vertically hanging cables that are attached at their upper ends to two giant cables, one on each side of the bridge, that form a *catenary*, or an upside-down arch (similar to the shape a rope or cable forms when held by its two ends).

Two towers hold up the massive cables. The cables are attached to anchors on the land at each end of the bridge. To support the bridge deck high above the water, the towers have to be very tall. The Golden Gate Bridge in San Francisco is a good example of a suspension bridge.

UNIQUE CHARACTERISTICS
See if you can spot where the giant cables are attached to their anchors at each end of the bridge. Attached to the giant cables are wire ropes and supports that form a walkway that allows bridge workers to walk to the tops of the towers. They don't climb up there without clipping

their safety belts onto the wire in case their feet slip. Beacon lights at the top of each tower warn aircraft of the structure's presence.

INTERESTING FACTS

The longest bridges in the world are suspension bridges. The Akashi Kaikyo Bridge, in Japan, is the longest at over 6,500 feet (1,990 m) — well over a mile. In the United States, the longest bridge is the Verrazano-Narrows Bridge between Brooklyn and Staten Island, at 4,260 feet (1,300 m). The center span of the Golden Gate Bridge is next longest; it's 4,200 feet (1,280 m) long.

The American Society of Civil Engineers named the Golden Gate Bridge one of the "Seven Wonders of the Modern World." The total bridge length is 4,600 feet (1,400 m). It connects San Francisco northward to Marin County. The towers rise 746 feet (227 m) above the bay, and the bridge deck is 220 feet (67 m) above the water. Each of its two suspended giant cables has a diameter greater than 1 yard (0.9 m), and is made up of a bundle of small, strong wires.

Cable-Stayed Bridge

BEHAVIOR
Spans moderately long rivers and costs less to build than a *suspension bridge* (see page 48).

HABITAT
Cable-stayed bridges are often confused with suspension bridges, but the two are really quite different. Currently there aren't many cable bridges around, but increasingly engineers are using this design. One of the better-known cable-stayed bridges is the Sunshine Skyway Bridge in Tampa, Florida. This bridge is so attractive that it won the prestigious Presidential Design Award from the National Endowment for the Arts.

HOW IT WORKS
Cables supporting the roadway connect directly to the bridge's tower or towers. Unlike suspension bridges, there are no catenaries, or suspended cables. Instead, the cables are drawn taut from the bridge deck to the tower. Suspension bridges have two suspended cables, but cable-stayed bridges have one set of cables attached directly to the tower from the center of the bridge, or from towers along the bridge.

INTERESTING FACTS
The Alex Fraser Bridge, which spans the Fraser River in British Columbia, Canada, was the longest cable-stayed bridge from 1986 (when it was built) until 2005. Now the Tatara Bridge in Japan is the longest, with a center span of 2,920 feet (890 m).

Floating Bridge

BEHAVIOR
Supports a road by floating on a lake or other body of water.

HABITAT
The bridge shown here crosses Lake Washington in Seattle, Washington. The lake, which was formed by glaciers during the last ice age, and is too deep for bridge supports to be sunk into the earth beneath it.

HOW IT WORKS
This is a rare type of bridge. The extensive maintenance it requires is justified only in places where the water is so deep and wide that neither a *suspension bridge* (see page 48) nor a bridge supported from the lake bed is feasible. The sections of bridge in shallow water are supported from footings in the lake bottom, but sections in deeper water float on large buoyant pontoons.

INTERESTING FACTS
Spanning 7,578 feet (2,310 m), Washington's Evergreen Point Floating Bridge (officially named the Governor D. Albert Rosellini Bridge—Evergreen Point) is the longest floating bridge in the world. Built in 1963, the bridge is due for replacement, but the potential costs of such an endeavor are staggering.

FIELDS AND STREAMS

THE TRAIL OF HUMAN TECHNOLOGY is visible almost everywhere, even in rural areas. To some degree, it's easier to spot in rural areas since human-made devices often stand out in contrast to nature.

Most of the technology visible in rural areas is associated with agriculture, communications, or resource extraction and transportation. But you can also see evidence of humans managing (or attempting to manage) nature. Keep your eyes peeled.

Fish Trap

BEHAVIOR

Biologists use fish traps to catch fish for tagging. *Fry*, or baby fish, are caught and have radio tags inserted into their bodies. Biologists also clip one fin from each fish before releasing the fry back into the stream. If the fish is caught again or if it passes through a radio sensor, the data is recorded so biologists know where it has traveled and how long it took to get there.

HABITAT

Fish traps are used in streams in those states that are studying fish populations. Contact your state fish and wildlife department to ask which streams are under study and where you can see a fish trap.

HOW IT WORKS

The flowing stream spins the fish wheel. Fish that swim into the wheel are trapped. As the wheel spins it lifts the fish up and deposits them into a screened cage in the water. Traps typically catch about 10 percent of the fish migrating downstream so biologists can tag them.

To tag the fish, a biologist inserts the tag into a syringe and injects it into the flesh of the fish. Fish tags are magnetic devices that have a unique 10-digit identification code. This code, along with the date and time that the fish was tagged, is recorded by passing the fish through a loop of wire that is an antenna for the recording device. Biologists also measure the size of the fish before releasing it.

When the fish passes through a similar loop at a dam or lock, radio equipment reads the identification number of the magnetic tag. This lets biologists estimate the number of fish that make their way into the ocean. Years later, when the fish returns to spawn in its native streams, biologists will record the identification number to get estimates of survival rates.

Watch the fish wheel of an operating trap spin. If biologists are working on the trap, approach and ask them questions.

INTERESTING FACTS

There are many kinds of fish traps. Native Americans used fish traps to catch fish for food. They set nets in a river and held them in place with poles. Fish would swim along the nets and into funnel-like openings in traps. Once inside a trap, fish are unlikely to venture out the small opening to escape. Native Americans then dip-netted fish from the congregated schools in the fish traps.

Today, traps can still be as simple as mesh nets mounted on poles in the river, or they may be more elaborate devices. Some use the river's gravitational energy to spin wheels like the one shown here to catch fish and move them into a collecting trap.

Fish Ladder

BEHAVIOR
Allows fish to swim past dams on rivers.

HABITAT
Dams and some locks have fish ladders if the rivers have fish, such as salmon, that migrate between the ocean and rivers. The ladders are located on one side of the river, near the bank.

HOW IT WORKS
Water is diverted at the top of the dam into a series of pools that reach from the top of the dam to the river's surface below the dam. Fish can swim "up the ladder" by swimming upward from one pool to another. They can stop and rest in a pool before continuing.

UNIQUE CHARACTERISTICS
Many fish ladders have windows designed to allow viewers to see the fish swimming in the pools. Of course, the fish don't migrate every month of the year, so you might not see any. But stop to check it out when you see signs announcing "fish ladder."

INTERESTING FACTS
One of the difficulties in designing a fish ladder is making sure that the fish can tell it's there. With no road maps to guide them, fish swim to the spot in the water where they think passage will be easiest. As part of their design plan, engineers must therefore include a way to direct the fish toward the ladder. The angle of the dam face relative to the river directs fish toward the ladder.

Stream-Gauging Station

BEHAVIOR
Houses equipment that measures the water level of a stream or a river.

HABITAT
On the banks of streams or on bridges that cross rivers.

HOW IT WORKS
A tube called a *stilling well* is anchored in the bed of the stream or river. A shelter is placed on top of the stilling well. Inside the shelter are the instruments that measure and record the water level.

The shelter houses a pulley with a metal wire that reaches down into the stilling well. A float at the end of the wire rests on the water's surface. As the level of water in the stream or river rises and falls, the float moves up and down, which causes the wire to move the pulley. The degree of movement of the pulley is recorded in a data logger (a device that keeps a record of data).

The stilling well features one or more pipes that let water in and out. This keeps the water level inside the stilling well at the same level as that of the stream or river. Waves don't interfere with the measurement, as the changes in water level that they cause don't pass through the pipes connecting the well to the river.

UNIQUE CHARACTERISTICS
A large measuring post, used to read the water level, is usually mounted on the outside of the well. Most stream-gauging stations now send the data back to laboratories by radio. Look for an antenna with short arms above the station.

INTERESTING FACTS
The United States Geological Service (USGS) operates about 7,000 stream-gauging stations throughout the country. Real-time stream flow conditions recorded by these stations may be viewed at http://waterdata.usgs.gov/nwis/rt.

Cableway Stream-Gauging Station

BEHAVIOR
Allows hydrologists (geologists who study water) to cross the river and measure its flow.

HABITAT
On deep or fast-moving rivers that have no bridge from which to take measurements.

HOW IT WORKS
Hydrologists travel a few feet along the cable in a cable car, and then lower a current-measuring device into the water. They record the measurement, then move to a new location along the cable to take another measurement.

They might make 25 measurements of a river's flow as they cross the river. At each location the water depth is also measured in order to calculate the volume of water flowing downstream each minute.

UNIQUE CHARACTERISTICS
Look carefully at the cable car, which is supported by a cable that is strung across the river. Would you like to cross a river in it? If so, consider becoming a hydrologist or a water engineer.

Insect Trap

BEHAVIOR
Traps are used to collect samples of insects or to kill harmful insects.

HABITAT
Hanging from trees in orchards and on farms.

HOW IT WORKS
There are several kinds of traps, each of which works differently. Many traps contain chemicals that lure specific insects, but not other bugs. The inside walls of these traps are coated with an adhesive that holds the insects in place once they land inside it. Other traps use food to entice insects. Sometimes the bait is covered with a chemical that coats the insects' breathing pores, killing them. Most traps are brightly colored to attract bugs and to make them easier to spot.

Electric Fence

BEHAVIOR
Provides a strong shock to anything or anyone that brushes up against it. Electric fences are used to keep domestic animals (mostly cattle) contained. To fence in animals as big and strong as cows or bulls, either a very strong fence or an electric fence is required. Electric fences are the less expensive of the two.

HABITAT
Electric fences are used on farms and ranches. You can tell that a fence is electric because at least one of the wires rests on an insulator (usually a white cylinder made of ceramic material) at each fence post. Without the insulator, the electric charge would run down the fence post to the ground, removing the electrical charge from the fence and making the fence ineffective.

HOW IT WORKS
The wire, which is supported by insulators, carries the electricity. The electricity isn't like the current in a wire that supplies electricity to your television or other appliance. It has a very short duration pulse of very high voltage. The fence system sends a pulse about once a second. Pulsing the electricity, instead of running it continuously, saves energy and money.

An animal brushing against the fence completes the electric circuit. The pulse of electricity runs from the fence to the animal and, through it, to the ground. Any animal feeling the pulse of electricity will move away. Experiencing the shock once or twice teaches animals, including humans, to avoid the fence.

INTERESTING FACTS
The voltages carried by electric fences range from 2,000 volts to 10,000 volts. Although the pulse lasts only a short time, it hurts. Stay away.

Wind Machine

BEHAVIOR
Stirs up the air to keep fruit or blossoms growing in an orchard from freezing.

HABITAT
These fans are used throughout the country wherever orchard or grove crops are harvested in cool weather. Florida growers protect their citrus crops with these.

HOW IT WORKS
As temperatures approach freezing, the fans turn on. As they spin they mix the cool and warm air that is present. This prevents very cold air, which is heavier than warm air, from settling on the ground in low-lying areas and causing freeze damage to blossoms or fruit on trees. Even the few degrees' change in what would otherwise be the ground temperature might be enough to save a harvest from frost damage.

Center Pivot Irrigation System

BEHAVIOR
Irrigates (supplies water to) crops.

HABITAT
Center pivot irrigation is used throughout the country, especially in the dry west. It works well in a large area (more than 40 acres, or more than 16.2 ha) that is devoted to a single crop.

HOW IT WORKS
This system includes its own propulsion. The pipes pivot around a central tower, their weight supported by wheels. A well or water pipe supplies water to the tower. Usually electric motors power the movement, but water pressure and gasoline engines are also used. By slowing down the rotation of the system, a farmer allows more water to blow onto the field. So, by adjusting the rate of rotation, farmers control the amount of water they apply.

UNIQUE CHARACTERISTICS
If you travel across the western United States by air, you can see large circles on the ground in some areas. The circles are irrigated lands that are watered by a center pivot irrigation system. Look at the color difference, from green to brown, between the irrigated circles and the adjacent land.

Traveling Big Gun Irrigation System

BEHAVIOR
Shoots water and fertilizer onto fields.

HABITAT
Small fields and fields that have uneven ground, which prohibits the use of a center pivot irrigation system.

HOW IT WORKS
The big gun uses water pressure of 90 to 125 pounds per square inch (6.3 to 8.8 kg/cm^2) to throw water a distance of up to 350 feet (107 m) onto a field. The hose is wound on a drum, which is mounted on a cart called a traveler. The cart also has a motor and pump to provide the water pressure. The hose nozzle is mounted on a smaller cart. Farmers set the nozzle cart away from the traveler. As fields are irrigated, the traveler slowly pulls the nozzle cart back.

The traveling big gun can be set up quickly, which is one of its chief advantages. A major disadvantage is that it requires someone to operate it. It is used on smaller plots of land (up to 30 acres, or 12 ha).

Side-Wheel Irrigation System

BEHAVIOR
Moves across a field, irrigating as it travels.

HABITAT
Level fields that are smaller than those in which a *center pivot irrigation system* (see page 62) is used or that feature heavy soil, which a center pivot system does not handle well.

HOW IT WORKS
Water is pumped through the pipes and out nozzles. The system can irrigate a swath of field that is about 60 to 90 feet (18 to 28 m) wide in one pass. A farmer then powers up a gasoline engine in the center section of pipe and "drives" the equipment to the next swath of land to be irrigated.

Pump and Stem Pipe Flood Irrigation System

BEHAVIOR
The pump draws water up from a well or other source and raises it into the stem pipe (white pipe pictured here), which distributes it to crops.

HABITAT
In fields that have crops planted in rows.

HOW IT WORKS
As the water level in the stem pipe rises, it flows out into the furrows (the trenches between rows of the crops) to irrigate the crops. Less water is lost to evaporation using this system than is lost by using irrigation systems that shoot water into the air to fall on crops. (This is especially effective in dryer climates such as Fresno, California, where this photograph of a pump and stem pipe system was taken.)

ON THE GROUND

IT'S NOT NECESSARY to climb a utility pole or dig underground to get quite close to roadside technology that is on the ground. Most sensitive equipment is hidden from view or located in hard-to-reach places, but there are many things you can bump into while walking around outside.

Like groundhogs burrowing through a field, underground wires and pipes have to come up to the surface occasionally, giving you the chance to see them. In neighborhoods that don't have overhead service delivery, cable, telephone, and electrical services come in from the ground. And gas, water, and sewer services come up from beneath the surface to enter houses and buildings. These are just some of the many interesting "what's that?" devices to discover on or near the ground.

Water Sampling Station

BEHAVIOR
Provides a way for technicians to draw samples of water from the water main. The water is tested for chlorine and other chemicals to make sure it is safe to drink.

HABITAT
Water sampling stations are located along water mains, which are usually located by roads. Typically they are about three to four feet tall and in the shape of a cylinder. There is a lock on the outside to prevent unauthorized people from drawing water.

HOW IT WORKS
Every few weeks someone will come by to draw a sample of water. The water is taken to a laboratory and a chemical analysis of the sample is performed. Contact the public works department of your city or county to find out where sampling stations are located and what chemicals the water is tested for.

Backflow Preventer

BEHAVIOR

Prevents water from traveling in the reverse direction in pipes. It is designed to stop potentially contaminated water from entering the water supply.

If the pressure decreased in a water pipe, water in the pipe could be sucked back into the city's water main. As the water moved back, it would suck surrounding, possibly contaminated, liquids into the system.

HABITAT

You can find backflow preventers virtually everywhere. Look for a pipe that rises out of the ground, travels a foot or so horizontally, and then goes back into the ground. You may see a valve on the horizontal pipe.

HOW IT WORKS

There are many different kinds of backflow preventers. Some act like one-way valves that let water flow from the source, but don't let water flow backward.

More common are "check valves" that let air in when the pressure drops. When water flows in the normal direction, the valve remains shut. When there is low pressure in the pipes, the valve opens, letting in air from outside. This breaks the suction in the pipe, preventing water from being sucked back into the main.

Water Valve Cover

BEHAVIOR
Protects the water valve that allows workers to shut off water that is in a main or flowing to a fire hydrant.

HABITAT
Water valves are buried in the streets and roads, and their covers are level with the road's surface. They are placed every few hundred feet along a water main and wherever a branch leaves the main to go to a neighborhood.

HOW IT WORKS
If workers need to service a fire hydrant (or shut it off after the bad guy's car crashes into it, as happens in all good movie car chases), they can remove the cover and turn the valve shut. To turn the valve they use a long-handled tool called a gate key, which fits into the top of the valve.

When you see a fire hydrant, look in the street to find the cover of the valve that cuts off its water supply. Once you spot one, see if you can find the adjacent ones in the road.

Why is a fire hydrant called a fireplug? It doesn't plug into a fire, does it? The name dates back a few hundred years, when firefighters in Europe tapped into wooden water mains to get water. To fight a fire, they would drill a hole into the wooden water main nearby and catch the water in buckets to douse the blaze. When the fire was out they stopped up the hole with a wood plug. Later, if another fire occurred at the same location, they didn't have to drill a new hole; they could simply remove the old plug to get water.

Storm Drain

BEHAVIOR
Collects rain and other water from the street and carries it to a stream, river, or holding pond.

HABITAT
Cities install storm sewers to keep the roads clear of water so cars can get through. Rural roads typically don't have storm drains and sewers. However, bridges do.

HOW IT WORKS
The street surface is angled so water will flow into a storm sewer. Water enters through an opening or a grate and falls into a catch basin. The basin collects solid materials (such as baseballs, quarters, and your report card) and keeps them from entering the pipes. As the water level rises in the basin it reaches and flows into a storm drain, which carries it to a nearby stream, river, or holding pond.

So will your baseball, quarter, or report card stay in the storm drain basin forever? Could there be a few thousand of them jammed in there? There could be if cities didn't clean out their storm drains. Most cities use giant vacuum trucks to remove all the solid stuff that falls into the drains.

The truck pumps water out at high pressure to dislodge material trapped in the storm drain or sewer. At the same time it sucks up the loosened material with a strong vacuum. If drains weren't cleaned out regularly, they would become clogged up and streets would flood, making it tough to get around.

Manhole Cover

BEHAVIOR

Keeps people, cars, and debris out of the sewer. The manhole provides access to the sewer so it can be cleaned.

HABITAT

Sewers run along streets and roads. A sewer is usually at least 10 feet (3 m) beneath the surface and is always below the water pipes so a sewer leak won't contaminate drinking water. Manholes and manhole covers are installed at intersections in the sewer system.

HOW IT WORKS

Manhole covers are heavy enough (approximately 100 pounds) to stay in place even as cars and trucks drive on them. However, very fast and low cars (Formula 1 race cars in particular) can suck manhole covers up into the air. To prevent accidents, the covers are anchored in place for races.

Made of cast iron, they are strong enough to support the weight of road vehicles. The covers fit into circular collars that are anchored in the concrete or asphalt road covering.

INTERESTING FACT

Most manhole covers now come from India.

Have you ever wondered why almost all manhole covers are round? The round shape prevents the cover from slipping through the opening and falling into the hole. A square or rectangular cover could fall in. Also, the cover weighs 85 pounds (40 kg) or more; its round shape allows workers to roll the cover along the street and into position instead of having to carry it.

Water Meter

BEHAVIOR

Measures how much water is used in a house or other building. In almost all cities residents pay for water based on how much they use. Cities measure water consumption with the meters and charge customers based on the reading of these meters.

HABITAT

Between a house or business's water main and the building itself. Businesses usually have meters behind the buildings. Residential water meters are located along property lines.

HOW IT WORKS

Water moving through the meter spins an *impeller* (a rotor designed to turn with the water flow). The impeller is connected to a series of gears that drive the counter that's visible on the face of the meter. As the flow of water increases the impeller spins faster.

UNIQUE CHARACTERISTICS

Some water meters are equipped with a radio transmitter that sends the water-use information to a recorder in a car or truck. (This type of meter has a wire sticking out of it.) Because they save time and money, cities are more and more frequently installing radio transmitters into existing water meters and are using them in new construction. Image how long it takes a meter reader to walk through every neighborhood in a town, find each meter, open it, read it, and record the numbers. With the radio transmitter system, the meter reader simply drives through a neighborhood; a computer data retrieval system inside a car or truck sends a message to each water meter, prompting it to send back its measurement, and the computer records all the data. Back at the water department, the data is downloaded and sent to the billing department, which sends out the monthly bills. What used to take several days of work now can be completed in a few hours with the radio system.

Gas Meter

BEHAVIOR

Measures and records how much gas is used in a house or business so the gas company can charge the user.

HABITAT

Communities that have gas service have gas meters.

HOW IT WORKS

The meter measures how much gas is used and displays the amount in cubic feet. Inside the box are two chambers, each of which is subdivided into two parts. The meter measures how many times gas fills and then empties from each of the chambers.

Look at the face of the meter to see if you can figure out how to read it.

Before someone digs near underground utilities, they need to call the utility company or companies to make sure that digging in that spot won't damage underground pipes or wires. Technicians are usually sent out to mark the ground above each utility company's buried pipes or wires. To help identify these markings, a standardized color code is used: yellow (natural gas or oil), red (electric), orange (telephone or cable), blue (water), and green (sewer).

Gas Valve Cover

BEHAVIOR
Protects a gas valve located below it. The valve allows sections of the gas line to be turned off if the line is damaged or needs repair.

HABITAT
Gas valves and their covers are located in streets. Look along streets that lead into residential areas.

HOW IT WORKS
Beneath the valve cover is a gate, or valve, that is used to shut off the gas service within an area. When the system needs to be shut down, a worker can turn the valve with a long-handled device called a gate key.

UNIQUE CHARACTERISTICS
The gas valve cover may feature the word "gas" on it. If it doesn't, it will have some other distinguishing feature so you can tell it apart from the nearby water valve covers.

> Do you know what natural gas smells like? If you have a gas stove, you've smelled the gas that escapes before the flame starts. If you can remember the smell, you might be surprised to know that natural gas is odorless.
>
> Has your nose deceived you? No. Natural gas is odorless and color-less. For this reason, it's pretty hard to detect. That's why gas companies add a smelly chemical, mercaptan, to the gas. It's the mercaptan you smell, not the gas itself. Without the smelly additive, you wouldn't know that gas is leaking.

Natural Gas Regulator

BEHAVIOR
It's part of a system that reduces the pressure in the gas lines.

HABITAT
Regulators are installed between high-pressure gas transmission lines and the lower-pressure gas lines that go to homes and businesses.

HOW IT WORKS
A hinged flapper provides escape for gas that is under excess pressure. There is a pressure-sensing device that operates the relief valve. The flapper opens to release gas and closes to keep out rain and debris. Sometimes there is a flag attached to the flapper that indicates that the flapper has opened.

UNIQUE CHARACTERISTICS
Adjacent to the relief valve is the regulator. The regulator reduces the pressure in the gas transmission line to a lower pressure used in the pipes that carry gas to homes and businesses.

Pipelines, both oil and gas, use pressure to move materials through the pipes. Natural gas moves through a pipe at about 15 MPH (24.1 KM/H) and oil moves at speeds of up to 5 MPH (8 KM/H). Friction along the inside walls of the pipes slows the material and reduces the pressure. To keep things moving, there are compressors (for gas) and pumps (for oil) every few miles along the pipeline.

One oil pipeline can carry kerosene, leaded gasoline, and unleaded gasoline at the same time. Each oil product is pumped into the pipeline in a batch (by itself), before or after the other products. The products are separated when they arrive at their destination.

Telephone Pedestal

BEHAVIOR
Houses the connections between one or more twisted pairs of copper wire that go into a house and the larger cable that runs from pole to pole.

HABITAT
In neighborhoods where telephone lines are located underground. Each pedestal serves two or more houses and is located along the property lines of the houses.

HOW IT WORKS
The front panel comes off (don't take it off yourself) so technicians can physically connect the pairs of wires and provide telephone service to a house.

UNIQUE CHARACTERISTICS
Although these boxes vary in size, most are about 8 to 10 inches (20 to 25 cm) square in diameter and 3 feet (0.9 m) tall, and they are usually green or gray in color.

Cross-Connection Box

BEHAVIOR
Houses devices that connect the telephone wires from a neighborhood to wires that run to a central office.

HABITAT
These gray-green metal cabinets are usually mounted on the ground, although they can be on utility poles.

HOW IT WORKS
Inside a cross-connection box are hundreds of connection points where technicians connect the twisted pair of wires from each telephone line in a neighborhood to other wires that carry the telephone signals to the central office. Often the wires running to the central office are carried underground.

UNIQUE CHARACTERISTICS
A cross-connection box may be mounted on a utility pole if it's in an area where there is a high chance for vandalism or where there isn't space on the ground for a box. This is called an aerial cross-connection box. You can identify it as a large metal cabinet with a platform in front of it for a worker to stand on. The cable coming out of the top of the aerial cross-connection box might go directly into a *splice box* (see page 192) mounted on the telephone cable.

Cable Pedestal

BEHAVIOR
Houses the connections between the television cable wires that run to homes and those that carry the signal to neighborhoods.

HABITAT
In neighborhoods that have underground wiring and cable television access.

HOW IT WORKS
The pedestal houses the connectors that technicians hook up in order to provide cable service to a home.

UNIQUE CHARACTERISTICS
The front of the pedestal may say "Cable TV," which is a good clue about what it's for. Cable pedestals are often located next to telephone pedestals.

Cable Vault

BEHAVIOR
Houses telephone or cable television splices.

HABITAT
In cities where service is provided underground.

HOW IT WORKS
Cable vault covers can be hinged or merely set in a collar set in the pavement. Workers can pry open the vault to make readings or adjustments.

UNIQUE CHARACTERISTICS
They're dangerous places to be. Harmful gases accumulate there, so don't pry up the lid and climb in.

Hand Hole

BEHAVIOR
Provides access to and protects cable splices, especially splices in optical fiber cables.

HABITAT
Adjacent to sidewalks or roads.

HOW IT WORKS
Hand holes provide access to wires underground, keeping them out of sight and safe from most environmental dangers. Service people can pull out the wires, splices, or other equipment inside a hand hole and test or repair it without having to climb utility poles.

Aerial Survey Marker

BEHAVIOR

Shows up in aerial photographs to assist surveyors in pinpointing the exact location of one place in the photo. It's the "you are looking here" mark for maps made from photographs taken from airplanes.

HABITAT

Almost anywhere an aerial survey may be performed. Aerial surveys are often done in areas that are about to be developed. Governmental agencies use aerial surveys to lay out cities and housing developments. Landowners use them to determine boundaries of their land.

Most commonly, aerial survey markers are painted on roads. Roads show up well in aerial photos and the large white symbols painted on the road make it easy to determine the exact location depicted in that part of the photo.

HOW IT WORKS

Aerial survey markers can be temporary (like the one shown in the photograph) or permanent (white lines painted on roads). Surveyors determine the exact locations of the markers and then use cameras mounted in airplanes to take photographs of the ground. The surveyors can measure distances on the photographs from the markers. Since they know the exact locations of the markers on the ground, the surveyors can figure out the exact location of other spots depicted in the photograph.

UNIQUE CHARACTERISTICS

The planes on which aerial photos are taken fly high to capture more area in a photograph and fly low to get more detail of a smaller area. Cameras on low-flying planes can capture images of small markers— these have arms that are about 4 inches (10 cm) wide and 25 inches (65 cm) long. Cameras in high-flying planes need larger markers—their arms may be up to 6 feet (2 m) long. The size of a marker can tell you if the survey plane is flying high or low.

Geodetic Control Station

BEHAVIOR

Shows where one of the four corners of a section of property is. For this purpose, property is divided into 1-mile (6-km) square sections. Each section's corners are marked with a control station brass cap. Thirty-six sections, in a square, form a township, which is the basic component of the property (land) system in the United States.

HABITAT

The brass caps that make up the geodetic control station are commonly called survey markers, and they're everywhere. However, they're not always easy to see. Sometimes you can spot one in a sidewalk or set in a rock in the woods.

HOW IT WORKS

Over the years surveyors have used a variety of techniques to find the exact locations where the control stations should be placed, but today they rely mostly on GPS. GPS stands for Global Positioning System, a satellite system that allows users to determine their exact location, or position, quite accurately.

The marker shown in this photo indicates that the land surrounding it was first surveyed in 1853, when the accuracy of a survey could be off by as much as a yard or a meter. Although getting within a yard or meter over a mile distance is pretty good, today surveyors can use GPS and pinpoint a location to within a few tenths of an inch. The location of markers in each county is recorded on a record of survey, which is filed with the local county auditor.

As is indicated in the photo, this location was resurveyed in 1940. Patos, the name stamped on the cap, is the location's name. This marker is on Patos Island, in the northwest corner of Washington.

Border Reference Monument

BEHAVIOR

Shows where the boundary is between the two countries. (The photo here was taken along the United States–Canada border.)

HABITAT

Along the international boundaries both north and south of the United States, and along the Alaska–Canada border. Where the boundary is in water, the monuments are set on land on opposite sides of the water, often a few miles apart. On land, smaller monuments are used. In rural areas a mile typically separates each nation's monuments from each other. They are closer to each other in urban areas.

HOW IT WORKS

These markers are obviously much larger and more prominent than the brass cap markers found throughout the United States. However, their positions are determined in the same way.

The photo here shows a GPS antenna set up over the monument on a tripod. Surveyors set up the antenna in order to check the position of the monument using GPS. The GPS instrument is in the yellow box shown on the ground beside the monument.

Railroad Signal Bungalow

BEHAVIOR
Houses and protects the electrical equipment that operates the bells, lights, and crossing arms at a railroad crossing.

HABITAT
Crossing signals are found wherever railway tracks cross busy roads. In the United States there are about 50,000 places where crossing signals are used.

HOW IT WORKS
Hundreds of yards from a railroad crossing, a sensor attached to the track activates when a train passes. This sensor consists of an electric circuit that a train completes as it runs over it. The signal produced by the electric circuit is detected inside the railroad signal bungalow and activates the crossing's warning bells and flashing lights. After enough time has passed for cars that are at the crossing to get out of the way, the railroad crossing arms are lowered. A second sensor detects the end of the train and that starts the opening process.

UNIQUE CHARACTERISTICS
Check out the crossing arms at a railroad crossing. They have a counter-weight on the short end to balance the weight of the long arm. This makes it easier for the motor to lift and lower the arm.

Railroad Manual Switch

Provides a method for a train to switch from one track to an adjacent track.

These switches are used throughout rail systems all over the world.

A railroad worker pulls a handle (hinged alongside the vertical bar) in one direction to move a special set of rails (called *points*) into position so that they connect the primary set of railroad tracks to a secondary, adjacent set of tracks. This allows a train to move to a different set of tracks in order to let another train approaching from the opposite direction pass, among other things. By pulling the handle in the other direction, the railroad worker removes the link to the secondary set of tracks, and trains continue along the primary set.

INDUSTRIAL SITES, BUILDINGS, AND THINGS ATTACHED TO BUILDINGS

BELOW ARE A FEW OF the more common or interesting industrial sites, buildings, and things attached to buildings you'll find along the road. There are so many types of sites that even experts can have a hard time identifying exactly what is manufactured by a plant just by looking at it from the outside. However, here are a few guidelines.

Buildings that have many loading docks for trucks could be warehouses or distribution centers. These are often located near interstate highways. Typically they are one story high, cover large areas, and have flat roofs with only a few vents in the roofs for air.

Multistory buildings with a variety of different-sized and -shaped vents are probably manufacturing plants. Smokestacks signify combustion (burning), which could mean the plant generates its own power or that it uses heat in processing materials. Large storage tanks suggest chemical processing plants. The presence of a rail line near the facility suggests the need for moving large quantities of raw materials or finished products.

High-tension wires signify either that the plant is producing power (see Electric Power Plants below) or that it uses a lot of electrical power. Aluminum plants are some of the biggest users of electricity and they are located where power is cheapest (for example, in the Northwest, where hydroelectric power is inexpensive).

A large parking lot for employees suggests labor-intensive manu-facturing, such as the assembly of components. One such example is the manufacturing of automobiles. Large plants often have a sign out front, so don't overlook the obvious hints, too.

ELECTRIC POWER PLANTS

Nearly all electric power plants convert mechanical power into electric power. The exceptions are plants that directly harness the sun's radiation. To supply the electricity that we use to light our homes, schools, and offices; heat our buildings; and power our appliances, there are about 2,500 power plants in North America.

In some types of plants, mechanical power is taken directly from nature. Hydroelectric plants use the natural water cycle, which carries water to high elevations and flows down toward the ocean by the pull of gravity. Along the way, power is extracted from the water. Falling water spins turbines that convert the gravitational power into electricity. Windmills generate electricity the same way, except that they use winds, not falling water, to spin the blades.

Most other plants use steam to spin turbines to produce electricity. *Geothermal plants* (see page 99) extract heat from the earth and use it to make steam. *Fossil fuel plants* (see page 91) burn coal, oil, or gas to heat water until it becomes steam. These fossil fuel plants contribute about 70 percent of the electric power in the United States.

Nuclear power plants (see page 97) use the heat produced in nuclear reactions to heat water. The process they use is called *fission*. It consists of splitting the nuclei of atoms into lighter elements. As the nuclei split, they release energy. About 13 percent of the electrical power in the United States is generated by nuclear plants.

Regardless of how heat is generated, it converts water into steam. The steam expands, exerting pressure on blades of giant turbines and causing them to spin. The spinning turbines spin generators that make electricity.

Generators are like electric motors, only in reverse. Motors take electrical energy and convert it into spinning mechanical energy. Generators take mechanical energy and convert it into electrical energy.

Power plants are easy to identify; they have high-voltage wires that carry electrical power away. Also, most power plants use heat to make steam and they require cooling towers. Fossil fuel plants require tons of fuel that is usually supplied via rail cars. (Check out the chapter "On Utility Poles and Towers" to see how the electricity gets from the power plant to your home.)

You can generate electricity with a small electric motor from a toy car (such motors can also be purchased at a hobby shop). Connect the motor terminals to a voltmeter that is set to read the lowest DC (direct current) voltages. Spin the motor shaft with your fingers and watch the voltmeter's needle move. The energy you generate by spinning the shaft is converted by the motor (generator) into electrical energy, which registers on the voltmeter.

If the voltmeter doesn't register any voltage, try spinning the motor shaft faster. Use a manual hand drill. Hold the motor shaft in the end of the drill where you'd normally put a drill bit. Have someone hold the motor and voltmeter while you turn the handle on the drill. (This works with an electric drill too, but should only be attempted in the presence of an adult.) You are using the energy you received from your most recent meal to make electricity.

FOSSIL FUEL POWER PLANTS

Fossil fuel power plants burn coal, oil, or natural gas to heat water until it becomes steam. The steam turns turbines that spin electric generators that produce electricity. Fossil fuel power plants are found throughout the United States and the world. You can identify a fossil fuel plant by the smokestack that raises the smoke away from the ground and people living nearby and allows the smoke to mix with the air higher up. Also, look for evidence of the fuel that's to be burned. Coal is usually shipped in long trains or river barges, so a coal-fired plant is adjacent to either many railroad tracks and coal cars or a dock for barges. Oil-fired plants have huge storage containers in the shape of cylinders. Gas can be stored in spherical or cylindrical tanks, but more often it comes directly from an underground pipeline.

Fuel is burned in a combustion chamber. Burning is a chemical reaction that releases heat. A boiler captures the heat and transfers it to water in pipes. The water heats up and becomes steam. The steam pushes on the blades of turbines, turning them. The spinning turbines spin electric generators that make electricity. After the steam has passed through the turbine, it is cooled and returned to the boiler. Cooling occurs in large cooling towers.

Although power plants remove most of the soot that results from burning the fuel, they still pollute the air. Check the smokestack to see how much material is being exhausted. Most of what you see is probably steam condensate (white rising plumes), but you may see other pollutants (darker coloration).

Gas-Fired Power Plant

BEHAVIOR
Burns natural gas to create steam, which is used to make electricity.

HABITAT
Throughout the United States.

HOW IT WORKS
Gas is piped into the plant through large pipes from gas wells, possibly far away. It is burned in furnaces that heat water in boilers. The high-pressure steam from the boilers spins turbines that drive electrical generators.

UNIQUE CHARACTERISTICS
You can identify a gas-fired plant in several ways. You will see high-voltage electrical wires leaving the plant. What you usually won't see is a source of fuel—or if you see it, you will only see the pipe. What you will not see are piles of coal, railroad cars, oil tankers, or oil tanks.

Gas-fired plants have smokestacks that are shorter than those of oil- and coal-fired plants. These stacks are shorter because burning gas produces fewer pollutants, so there's less of a need to get the pollutants high in the air.

Coal-Fired Power Plant

BEHAVIOR
Burns coal to generate electricity.

HABITAT
Coal-fired plants exist throughout the United States, especially in the East and the Midwest, where hydroelectric power isn't available.

HOW IT WORKS
Like other fossil fuel power plants (which burn oil or gas), coal-fired power plants burn the fuel to heat water until it becomes steam. The steam turns the blades on turbines, and the turbines spin electrical generators to create electricity.

UNIQUE CHARACTERISTICS
Most existing coal-fired plants have smokestacks that are exceptionally tall. Many are 1,000 feet (300 m) tall. Their height allows their emissions—sulfur dioxide and other chemicals responsible for acid rain—to disperse over a wide area. Shorter stacks would allow the emissions to concentrate in the area near the power plant, polluting local waters. Taller stacks get the emissions up high where winds are stronger and where the emissions can mix with clean air and spread out. New coal plants are designed to have shorter stacks because they will have *scrubbers*, devices that remove most of the particulate matter (the pollutants) that comes from combustion.

Look for a major rail line going into the plant to supply coal. Large coal-fired plants burn so much coal that they need to have it delivered by the trainload.

Oil-Fired Power Plant

BEHAVIOR
Burns fuel oil to generate electricity.

HABITAT
Throughout the United States.

HOW IT WORKS
Oil is burned in a furnace that heats water until it becomes steam. The steam turns turbine blades that are connected to an electrical generator, which creates electricity.

UNIQUE CHARACTERISTICS
Oil-fired plants have large oil tanks that store the oil. Although their smokestacks are taller than those at gas-fired plants, they are much shorter than those at coal-fired plants.

Hydroelectric Power Plant

BEHAVIOR
Generates electricity via water that falls from high elevations. Rivers are dammed to collect the water in valleys to provide a steady source of water to run the plants' turbines.

Not all dams have electrical generation stations. Some dams store water for dry times of the year; some divert water into irrigation canals or drinking water systems; and some prevent floods by collecting storm waters.

HABITAT
For hydroelectric generators to be effective, water must fall down from high elevations that have abundant rainfall or snowfall. The mountains of the western United States, particularly those in the Pacific Northwest, are ideal for generating hydroelectric power.

HOW IT WORKS
Power companies construct a dam to hold water in mountain valleys. Water drains from the surrounding land as rains fall and as snow melts, filling the reservoir behind the dam. Water can escape by running through large tubes called *penstocks* down to a generating station. The pressure of water falling from the height of the dam to the turbine far below turns the blades of turbines. Spinning turbines turn generators that make electricity.

UNIQUE CHARACTERISTICS
Look for the generating plant below the face of the dam. Near the plant will be a substation, where the voltage of the electricity generated is transformed into much higher voltages. These voltages are carried by the wires running from the plant to distant users.

INTERESTING FACTS
The 1,000 hydroelectric plants in the United States supply about 13 percent of the country's electricity.

Wind Turbine/Generator

BEHAVIOR
Converts mechanical energy (from wind) into electrical energy.

HABITAT
You see wind turbines in locations that have steady winds of about 10 mph (16 км/н). Faster winds can damage the equipment and slower winds aren't strong enough to produce electricity. The generators run efficiently when the winds blow steadily.

Even a few years ago it was rare to see a wind farm. However, recent advances in technology have lowered the cost of building and maintaining windmills. Today, electric utilities are building wind farms. A *wind farm* is a power-generating plant that uses wind power. You can find wind farms in many states. Large wind farms are located in the passes of the coastal mountains of California and along the Columbia River in Oregon and Washington. Wind resource maps for states are available on the Department of Energy's Web site at www.eere.energy .gov/windandhydro/windpoweringamerica/wind_maps.asp.

HOW IT WORKS
As wind blows through the blades of a windmill, it exerts pressure on the blades, spinning them. The blades are attached to a shaft. On most windmills the shaft is connected to a gearbox, which houses gears that increase the rate of rotation. The gears spin an electric generator that makes electricity.

UNIQUE CHARACTERISTICS
Where you see one windmill you are likely to see many. It is cost effective to site many of them together.

Nuclear Power Plant

BEHAVIOR
Uses nuclear fuel to create nuclear fission. The heat generated turns water into steam, the steam drives turbines, and the turbines spin generators to create electricity.

HABITAT
There are more than 100 nuclear power plants operating in the United States. Most of them are found along the eastern seaboard and in the Midwest.

HOW IT WORKS
Fissionable material, usually uranium, is placed in the reactor. As the uranium atoms split (fission), they emit high-energy particles and they also release energy as heat.

Nuclear reactions are changes that occur in the nuclei of very heavy metals such as uranium and plutonium. Fission is one type of nuclear reaction; the others are radioactive decay and fusion.

Fission is the splitting of heavy nuclei into lighter materials. To produce fission, neutrons bombard the uranium or plutonium, splitting some of its atoms and releasing energy as radiation and heat.

UNIQUE CHARACTERISTICS

You can identify most nuclear power plants from other plants by their dome-shaped or cylindrical-shaped containment buildings. The containment buildings are made of concrete and have no openings. The reactor is inside the containment building.

Boiling water reactors house the containment structure inside another building so you can't see it. At a boiling water reactor you will see a rectangular turbine building with a square reactor building behind it. About one third of the reactors in the United States are of this type.

In addition to the domed roof of the containment vessel, look for the giant cooling tower, which is the plant's most conspicuous feature. Nuclear power plants generally use "natural draft" cooling towers such as the 350-foot-tall (107-meter-tall) towers shown in this photo. However, as you can see in the photo, the coal-fired plant in the background also uses natural draft cooling towers.

Nuclear power plants require a large, reliable source of water to use in their cooling towers. For this reason, they are always located near a body of water such as a river, lake, or ocean.

Another distinguishing feature of all nuclear reactors is the absence of a smokestack. Generating plants that burn fossil fuels have tall smokestacks with smoke coming out. At a nuclear power plant you might see water vapor rising above the cooling tower, but you won't see smoke.

INTERESTING FACTS

There are 103 operating nuclear power plants in the United States, about a quarter of the total in the world. In the United States, nuclear power contributes about 13 percent of the country's electricity. However in some states, such as Vermont, South Carolina, New Hampshire, and Illinois, nuclear power is the primary source of electric power.

Geothermal Power Plant

BEHAVIOR
Uses naturally occurring underground pockets of heat to produce electricity.

HABITAT
In the United States geothermal power plants are located mostly in California, other western states, Hawaii, and Alaska.

HOW IT WORKS
These power plants use underground steam that is generated when water comes into contact with hot rocks. The heat of the rocks is a product of geothermal energy, the naturally occurring radioactive decay of material in Earth's core. The steam drives turbines that spin electrical generators, which create electricity.

Water from underground springs is heated by the hot rocks. Sufficient heating transforms the water into steam. Power companies drill into the earth's surface to tap pockets of steam so they can pipe it to the surface.

In areas where there isn't enough water underground, companies will pump surface water down into the hot pockets under the earth. The water heats and changes to steam, and the steam is withdrawn to drive the turbines.

UNIQUE CHARACTERISTICS
High-tension wires leaving the plant indicate that the structure is a power plant. If there is no obvious source of energy, such as tanks of oil, gas lines, or long trains carrying coal, the structure might be a geothermal plant. Unlike many other plants, geothermal power plants don't burn anything, so they don't have smokestacks. Most geothermal plants are located in the western states and in Hawaii and Alaska, so the location of the structure is also a clue.

INTERESTING FACTS
Geothermal power is renewable. As long as the radioactive materials in the earth's core decay, the earth will generate heat that we can capture and convert into electricity.

Step-Up Transformer

BEHAVIOR
Increases the voltage from about 15,000 volts to between 150,000 and 765,000 volts for long distance transmission.

HABITAT
Step-up transformers are found next to power plants. The power plants produce electricity at between 15,000 and 20,000 volts. However, electricity at this voltage will sustain resistive losses as it travels long distances through the wires. To reduce the losses, it is "stepped up" to a much higher voltage.

HOW IT WORKS
Transformers can be designed to either increase or decrease the voltage of an alternating current. Inside transformers, wires are wrapped around a hollow core made of steel or iron. In a step-up transformer, wires from a generator are wrapped around one side. Wires that take the higher-voltage electricity away are wrapped around the other side. If both sides had the same number of wrappings, or windings, there would be no change in the voltage. However, the output side has 10 or more times the number of windings that the generator side has. This increases the voltage 10 or more times.

Electricity applied to the first side creates (by induction) a magnetic field. That is, the alternating electrical current generates a magnetic field. The magnetic field creates an electric current in the second side. The strength of the electric field varies directly with the number of windings.

UNIQUE CHARACTERISTICS

Big transformers are filled with oil and have fans to cool them. See if you can follow the wires from a power plant to its transformer and out to the high-voltage wires that carry the electricity away. You can identify the transformer as a large, rectangular structure with cooling fins on the sides, attached fans, and wires connected.

INTERESTING FACTS

You may know that the voltage in your house is 120 volts. Since the voltage produced by the power plant is between 15,000 and 20,000 volts, and if that voltage is greatly increased when it is transmitted, there must be someplace where the voltage is reduced.

Actually, there are a couple of places where it is reduced. The first occurs at a substation; the second is on the utility pole outside your house. The first lowers the voltage to a safer level and the second lowers the voltage to levels usable in your home.

Electric Power Substation

BEHAVIOR

Reduces the high voltages of electricity carried by long-distance wires to voltages carried by wires on utility poles, then distributes the electrical power. It also has circuit breakers and switches that allow the substation to be disconnected from the grid when workers need to perform maintenance work on the station.

HABITAT

Every town or region has one or more substations. Sometimes they are difficult to see, as electric companies camouflage them. Look for high-tension wires supported by large metal towers, and a high chain-link fence surrounding the towers.

HOW IT WORKS

A substation's main task is to reduce the voltages carried by long transmission lines. Transmission wires carry electricity at very high voltages (several hundred thousands volts). The wires that run through neighborhoods and business areas carry electricity typically at 7,200 volts. Substations reduce the voltages of the electricity in the transmission lines and distribute the lower-voltage power.

Wires from a lower-voltage side (distribution wires carried by utility poles, typically 7,200 volts) are wrapped around a hollow core made of steel or iron. Wires from the transmission side (voltage carried by transmission wires, which carry electricity of much higher voltages—usually several hundred thousand volts) are wrapped around the other side of the core. The transmission side of the core has several times the number of windings as does the lower voltage side to reduce the voltage.

Electricity applied by the transmission wires creates a magnetic field. The magnetic field creates an electric current in the second side of the core. The strength of the electric field varies directly with the number of windings of each set of wires.

UNIQUE CHARACTERISTICS

Chain-link fences surround substations to prevent people from getting near the dangerous equipment. But through the fence you can see giant switches and circuit breakers. Trace the flow of power from the incoming transmission lines to the transformers and out the other side to the local distribution system.

It's interesting to note that the substation itself has to have power to run. It gets its power from a set of wires from the lower-voltage, or output, side. You may be able to see the smaller electric wires coming from a nearby utility pole back into the substation to provide it with power.

The electric current that flows through the transformers generates considerable heat. When the transformers get too hot, fans mounted on their sides are activated and blow air across them. If you see fans inside a substation, you know you're looking at transformers.

Electric Fuse

BEHAVIOR
Protects equipment from surges in electricity or from dangerously large currents.

HABITAT
Fuses are used in *electric power substations* (see page 102) and on some utility poles. They are foot-long (30-cm), thin cylinders mounted with insulators at each end. You can see a wire coming in to the upper connection to the fuse and another wire leaving from the bottom connection.

HOW IT WORKS
Fuses are designed to burn out quickly before other, more expensive equipment is damaged. Inside, a thin wire carries the electric current. When a surge occurs, the increased current flows through the fuse. Resistance in the wire causes it to heat up as the current rises, and the increasing heat melts the wire. The wire breaks, disrupting the flow of the current before the surge damages other equipment.

INTERESTING FACTS
Fuses protect a wide variety of electrical devices. Your car has fuses (usually located underneath the dashboard), and many electrical appliances have them as well. (The electric story continues in Chapter 9.)

Power plants generate alternating current. In the United States the current alternates 60 times a second. If you could measure the current very quickly you would find that it forms a wave of positive and negative voltages 60 times a second. Electrons in a wire move forward and then backward 60 times a second.

In most cases, any electricity that is wired into a home features an alternating current. The electricity produced by a battery features direct current. The electric power in a flashlight, for example, has a direct current.

Natural Draft Cooling Tower

BEHAVIOR
Cools the water used to remove heat from electrical power-generating plants so the water can be used again as coolant.

HABITAT
These massive cooling towers are used at very large power plants. Most nuclear power plants use this type of cooling system.

HOW IT WORKS
The tower acts like a giant radiator. Hot water from the power plant is pumped into the cooling tower and sprayed onto a series of platforms. Air comes into the tower through the large openings at the tower's base. As the air moves up through the water spray, it picks up heat and evaporates some of the water (about 3 percent). In this way, heat is removed from the water and transferred to the air. The warm air rises and pulls more cool air into the tower from the vents at the bottom. This flow of air caused by the transfer of heat, is called *convection*. For this reason, these towers are sometimes called convection cooling towers.

UNIQUE CHARACTERISTICS
Most natural draft cooling towers are as tall as 500 feet (152 m) and as wide as 400 feet (122 m) in diameter at the base. From the broad base, the tower narrows and then widens again at the top. The shape improves the convection, or upward circulation, of air. The towers are so tall that they have to feature lights to warn aircraft of their presence.

Look for the white clouds of water vapor (not smoke) rising above natural draft cooling tower.

Mechanical Draft Cooling Tower

BEHAVIOR
Cools water used in power-generating plants and other plants. The water is then recirculated to the plant for use again.

HABITAT
Mechanical draft cooling towers are found in many industrial parks and on some campuses that have many buildings. They are more common than the larger, natural draft cooling towers.

HOW IT WORKS
Water that's been heated by the production of power is pumped into the tower and into pipes that spray the water inside. Fans pull air up past the falling water. Heat is removed from the water when it comes in contact with the cooler air and by evaporation (some of the water turns into water vapor, which removes heat as well).

UNIQUE CHARACTERISTICS
The air moving through a cooling tower gains water vapor. On cold days this vapor condenses back into tiny water droplets above the tower. You can see these clouds on cold days, but you are less likely to see them when it's warm.

INTERESTING FACTS
Mechanical draft cooling towers use evaporative cooling. You experience evaporative cooling when you get out of a shower, bath, or swimming pool. In a dry climate, water evaporates quickly, which can chill you.

Oil Refinery

BEHAVIOR
Converts oil into products such as gasoline, diesel and jet fuel, heating oil, lubricants, and raw material for other petrochemical products.

HABITAT
Near seaports and other sources of oil (such as oil pipelines and wells). Much of the oil used in the United States travels by tanker or barge from oil rigs located out in the ocean and is pumped ashore to refineries.

HOW IT WORKS
A refinery separates oil into its different parts. Oil is composed of many long-chained molecules that have to be segregated so they can be used for different purposes. In the refinery, the oil is heated, turning much of it into vapors. The vapors rise in a tall column, and as they cool they condense, or turn back into liquid. Each part, or component, condenses at a different rate. Lighter components, such as gasoline, for example, rise to the top of the column before condensing. As the different parts condense, they are collected. Each component is then treated with chemicals to improve its usefulness.

UNIQUE CHARACTERISTICS
Refineries stand out among industrial plants because of their mazes of pipes and tanks. Huge storage tanks hold oil waiting to be refined, as well as refined products waiting to be shipped out. The pipes move the oil through the several stages of refining.

Wastewater Treatment Plant

BEHAVIOR

Cleans the wastewater from houses and businesses and returns it to rivers and streams. Imagine a machine that takes the water flushed down a thousand toilets and makes it clean enough to pump back into a river where fish can live. That's what a wastewater treatment plant does.

HABITAT

Every city and town has at least one facility or shares a facility with another city or with their county. The plants are located on low-lying land, near rivers or other bodies of water.

HOW IT WORKS

Sewage flows into the plant through large pipes called sewers. The first part of the plant is called the *headworks*. This is where water runs through grates to remove any large objects and inorganic material (metal or plastics).

After the headworks process comes secondary treatment. Microbes (bacteria) are encouraged to consume the organic materials (waste). The wastewater is moved continuously and oxygen or air is pumped through it to support the microbes. Then the water is pumped into *clarifiers*.

Clarifiers are large round tanks that have mechanical sweep arms that continuously move through the wastewater. Solids in the wastewater fall to the bottom, and the lighter, cleaner water spills over the top of the clarifiers. The clean water is then moved to another vessel, where it undergoes disinfection, the third stage in the process.

Increasingly, disinfection is done with ultraviolet lights. The lights are inserted into pipes that the water flows through. The lights kill all the microbes. Then the water can be released into a river. (Before plants started using ultraviolet lights, chlorine was used to disinfect the water. However, chlorine itself has to be removed so that it doesn't kill the microbes and fish that naturally occur in rivers. If you have a fish tank you probably have to treat tap water to remove the chlorine in it before you put the water into your aquarium.)

The sludge (solids mixed with some water) that falls out of the water in secondary treatment can be filtered through sand to remove the solids. All the solid materials are dried and hauled away to a land-fill or composting facility.

UNIQUE CHARACTERISTICS
Wastewater treatment plants have several distinct features. They take up a lot of room. They have several large pools of water that are either open to the air or are covered with metal dome roofs. They have many pipes to move water.

Until recently, you could identify a plant by the smell of sewage. However, today environmental regulations require plants to release almost no unpleasant odors.

INTERESTING FACTS
Many wastewater treatment plants will be happy to give you a tour. Don't be squeamish—dive in!

Lift Station

BEHAVIOR

Lifts sewage, prompting the wastewater to flow downhill to the wastewater treatment plant. Wastewater flows by gravity from homes and businesses to the treatment plant. To keep the wastewater moving, the pipes must be angled downward from the source to the plant. Because wastewater often travels several miles to reach the treatment plant, it doesn't begin its journey at ground level. If it did, even a small downward angle would mean that the sewers would end up being very deep underground once they reached the treatment plant. Instead, lift stations raise the wastewater and let it flow downward in pipes that are closer to the surface of the ground. They are also used to lift sewage up and over hills that may separate the homes and businesses producing the sewage and the sewage treatment plant.

HABITAT

On government-owned land. Unless you look hard, you won't see one. Sometimes you can see pipes rising from the ground, but more often all that's visible are concrete buildings with no windows.

HOW IT WORKS

Wastewater flows into the lift station underground. There, any large debris is removed and the remaining sewage passes through a pump. The pump sends it upward through pipes so it can flow out and down to either the next lift station or the treatment plant.

Since the sewage must flow even during a power outage, most lift stations have emergency diesel-powered generators. If electrical power fails, the generator can start automatically to generate electricity to run the pumps.

Because there is raw sewage flowing through the lift station, the air inside the station can smell bad. For this reason, the air is pumped through activated carbon, which absorbs odors, or through a scrubber, which sends water and chemicals falling through the air to remove the odors. The treated air is pumped outside through vents. But even with chemical scrubbers, lift stations can emit a slight odor that identifies their function.

UNIQUE CHARACTERISTICS
You might see a small vent pipe in a lift station's walls; this allows the exhaust from the diesel generator to leave the building.

Lightning Rod

BEHAVIOR
Protects buildings from being hit by lightning by carrying the electrical energy of a lightning strike to the ground. When lightning hits buildings, it can damage them and start fires.

HABITAT
Buildings, barns, and homes. They are more prevalent in regions that have more lightning. In the United States, which is hit by about 90 million lightning strikes each year, the areas with most lightning-caused injuries include Florida, Michigan, Pennsylvania, North Carolina, and New York.

HOW IT WORKS
The lightning rod system conducts electricity. The components are made of metals that have low resistance to electrical current. Lightning seeks the path of least resistance toward the ground and follows the lightning rod and its wire.

Lightning can damage a lightning rod, but a rod is easy and inexpensive to repair compared to the effort and expense involved in repairing or replacing a building.

UNIQUE CHARACTERISTICS
Although some lightning rods are ornate, the typical rod is simply a straight metal pole that is attached to the roofline of a building. Attached to the rods is a heavy-duty wire, which runs down the length of the building and is attached to a metal grid buried in the ground nearby.

> Benjamin Franklin invented lightning rods after his famous kite experiment. Don't try flying a kite during an electric storm, as it is quite dangerous. Lightning kills about 100 people in the United States alone each year.

High-Rise (Tower) Crane

BEHAVIOR
Hoists building materials from the ground up to the part of a building that is under construction.

HABITAT
These are used to construct buildings that are at least several floors tall. Since this type of building is most commonly found in cities, that's where you usually see tower cranes.

HOW IT WORKS
A high-rise crane "grows" with the building. The crane is lifted into place by another crane that is mounted on a truck.

Once a high-rise, or tower, crane is set up, it can be made taller by inserting a new section of tower into it. A hydraulic jack holds onto the base of the crane and jacks up the top part so a new section can be inserted into the crane. Workers bolt the new section into place and remove the jack. When workers are ready to do construction on even higher levels of the building, the jack picks up the crane so yet another section can be inserted.

Notice the large counterweight at the short end of the crane's arm. Without a counterweight, the crane would have to be made much stronger to support itself and hold the heavy weight of construction materials.

High-rise cranes are often built inside a future elevator shaft. When they are removed the shaft is ready for elevators to be installed.

UNIQUE CHARACTERISTICS
Look to see if there is a worker in a cab near the top of the crane. If not, look on the ground for a worker who is running the crane with a large remote control box.

Gas Station Pump

BEHAVIOR
Dispenses gasoline and diesel fuel for cars and trucks.

HABITAT
At gas stations throughout the world.

HOW IT WORKS
When gas stations were new, the "pump" had a pump inside to pull the gasoline up from underground tanks and push it into the tank of a car. Newer gas dispensers don't have a pump inside them, but rely instead on a pump near the storage tanks. This pump builds pressure in the storage tanks, causing the gasoline to flow up to the dispenser—the gas is pushed into the car's tank, not sucked up into it. Listen to the dispenser for the sound of a pump starting. If you don't hear a pump, the dispenser doesn't have one.

UNIQUE CHARACTERISTICS
Watch for large tanker trucks filling up the underground tanks at gas stations. See if they measure the depth of fuel in the tanks with a giant "yard" stick.

How does the gas pump know when to shut off? Check out the end of the nozzle to see a small hole (or holes) and a tube leading from the hole into the handle. As gas flows through the nozzle, a suction pump turns on and sucks air through the hole and the tube. The airflow stops when the level of gas in the tank reaches the level of the hole. That suddenly increases the suction pressure in the tube. The change in pressure pulls a mechanical linkage that shuts off the pump.

Hydraulic Lift

BEHAVIOR
Lifts automobiles off the ground so mechanics can get underneath them to do maintenance.

HABITAT
In most service stations and on aircraft carriers (navy ships that launch and land airplanes), which use giant lifts to move planes from the hangar deck to the flight deck. In addition, elevators in some low-rise buildings use similar devices.

HOW IT WORKS
A piston is forced up by pressure and rises from an underground cylinder. The cylinder is filled with oil under pressure. To raise the lift, the oil pressure in the cylinder is increased. Often you will hear the pump on the lift's compressor start up as the lift rises. The compressor pumps air into a tank that increases the pressure on the oil inside the tank. The attendant lets some of this pressurized oil into the cylinder to lift the car. When the air pressure in the tank drops, the compressor starts pumping again. To keep the oil from escaping out of the cylinder, there is a "wiper seal" at the top of the cylinder.

The lift works on the principle of hydraulics. The pressure (force per area) in a closed system is the same everywhere in that system. A small force in a small pipe can provide the same pressure as a larger force in a large pipe. A small force can raise a larger one (like the weight of a car) provided the smaller force is exerted in a smaller pipe.

UNIQUE CHARACTERISTICS
As a lift is operating, listen for the compressor to start. As the lift rises it uses energy that is stored in a tank as pressure. The compressor begins to pump when the pressure in the tank falls below a specified level.

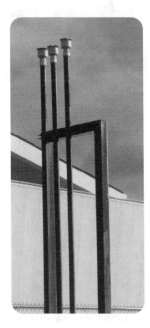

Underground Tank Vent Pipes

BEHAVIOR
The pipes let excess air escape from underground tanks that store gasoline, and they let air into the tanks as gasoline is pumped out.

HABITAT
Gas stations. Look behind or toward the back of a gas station for a stand of several vertical pipes, each about 15 feet (4.6 m) tall.

HOW IT WORKS
Permits air to enter and leave the tank as its volume of gasoline changes.

Water Storage Tank

BEHAVIOR
Holds water and maintains water pressure in the pipes that go to homes and businesses.

HABITAT
In an area with hills, water tanks are located at or near the tops of hills. In flat terrain they can be located anywhere, but they need to be elevated on long steel legs. Water storage tanks that are on these tall legs are called water towers.

HOW IT WORKS
Water is pumped into the storage tank until the tank is nearly full. As people use water, the water level in the tank falls. When the water falls to a certain level a switch inside the tank is automatically activated. The switch turns the pumps on to refill the tank. Tanks are elevated on long legs or sit on hill tops so the water inside can flow through pipes to users below.

UNIQUE CHARACTERISTICS
Because a tank has to be maintained and cleaned every few years, it features a ladder leading to the top, where there is an opening for maintenance workers to get inside the tank. In some cases, the tank is drained before it is cleaned. For this reason, you might also see a plug near the bottom of the tank. Some cities employ scuba divers to clean the insides of the tanks, however, so there is no need to drain these tanks.

Tanks have measuring sticks that are visible from the outside of the tank. This allows technicians to measure the depth of the water inside a tank without having to get inside it.

6 ANTENNAS

ANTENNAS RECEIVE AND TRANSMIT radio signals that carry radio, television, telephone, and radar signals. The size, shape, and location of an antenna can indicate its function. The size also gives you an estimate of the size of the signal (called the wavelength, or the length of the radio wave) it is designed to capture. An antenna must be at least one-fourth as long as the wavelength of the signal it sends or receives. Thus you can guess that cell phones, which have antennas that are only a few inches in length, must receive very short wavelength signals. Amateur-radio antennas can be 100 feet (30 m) long; they pick up radio waves that equal the length of a football field.

Antennas are classified into two groups. *Wire antennas* include radio antennas on cars, antennas on cell phones, antennas inside radio receivers, and antennas for television.

The other group is *aperture antennas*. These are antennas with an opening, or an *aperture*. They include dish antennas used to receive television signals from satellites and microwave antennas used to send and receive telephone calls from landline (wired) phones.

One type of aperture antenna is the *parabolic antenna*. This type is shaped like a curved dish. It captures radio signals and focuses them to a single point. The larger the dish, the more signal energy it can pick up. Older satellite television antennas, which are still frequently seen mounted on homes, are large (3 feet, or 0.9 m, or larger across the dish) because these satellites are sending signals at low power. Newer dish antennas are only 18 inches (46 cm) across, because the newer satellites transmit more powerful signals. To receive the faint signals from distant satellites in outer space, NASA uses parabolic antennas that are up to 200 feet (60 m) across.

Most dish antennas don't move. They face a satellite that is in *geosynchronous orbit*—the satellite turns as fast as the earth spins, so it stays in one place relative to Earth. Many dish antennas receive signals from the same satellite, and each of them points directly at that satellite. Dish antennas that do move have visible motors. This type of antenna also has sensors to tell the computer controlling the position of the antenna where it is pointing. Astronomers use moving antennas so they can collect radio signals from different areas of the sky.

Amateur-Radio Antenna

BEHAVIOR
Transmits and receives radio waves.

HABITAT
In homes, universities, and even cars around the world. There are nearly 700,000 amateur-radio operators (called hams) in the United States, and about two million more throughout the rest of the world. Although hams use a variety of different antenna sizes and types, a wire strung from one house to another or from a house to a tree is commonly used.

HOW IT WORKS
There are several different types of amateur-radio antennas. This photo shows a four-element Yagi (named for its inventor) antenna sitting atop a retractable tower that is in a nested (or low) position.

Hams operate radio receivers and transmitters to talk to fellow hams around the world. They communicate using Morse code (a system of dots and dashes) or voice. A ham selects a wavelength to use for transmitting messages and sends out a call, which may be picked up by anyone, anywhere listening on that wavelength. The long antennas allow hams to use long wavelength radio waves that travel farther than shorter wavelengths.

UNIQUE CHARACTERISTICS
To get the long wavelength signals out from a car, hams use large whip antennas, which are much longer than car radio antennas. Often they show their call signs (numbers and letters) on their license plates or on signs attached to their cars. In the United States, look for license plates that start with the letter "W," then may feature another letter, then a digit (that represents the area of the country), then three more letters.

> Why are amateur radio operators called hams? Ham is an abbreviation for amateur, with the hard sound of "H" added to make it easier to detect. So they are called "hams," not "ams."

Microwave Antenna

BEHAVIOR
Some older systems send and receive analog (as opposed to digital) communications, but newer systems relay communications digitally.

HABITAT
This type of antenna is used to carry telephone signals over long distances where it would be too expensive to run telephone wires or cable. You often see them adjacent to interstate highways in rural areas. They are also found on cellular telephone towers, where they transmit telephone messages to a central office far away.

HOW IT WORKS
Telephone conversations are converted into digital signals and are transmitted as microwaves, or very short-wavelength radio waves. One microwave antenna transmits signals to the next antenna. These can travel as far away as 40 miles (64 km), but typically the distance between antennas is 25 miles (40 km). One antenna has to have an unobstructed line of sight to the next one. For this reason, microwave antennas are located on towers or on hilltops.

UNIQUE CHARACTERISTICS

Microwave antennas are generally covered bowls. They range in size from 2 to 12 feet (0.6 to 3.7 m) across. Some older systems (now found only in rural areas) may use an antenna that looks like a flyswatter.

Why are they covered? Often a hard, but not metallic, rounded cover is placed over the entire dish to protect the feed horn (the part that radiates the signal) from strong winds, falling objects such as ice that may form higher up on the tower, and birds that decide to build a nest on it. The feed horn is generally not as rugged as the dish itself, and the position of the end of the feed horn is critical to the proper operation of the antenna, making it important to protect.

Wavelength is one way to measure a radio, or electromagnetic, wave. Radio, television, radar, and cell telephone signals travel as invisible waves that move at the speed of light (186,000 miles, or 299,388 km, per second). Wavelength describes how far apart the crests of the waves are. Antennas can pick up waves as short as a fraction of an inch (these are called microwaves) and waves as long as 100 feet (30 m).

Different-sized wavelengths are used to do different things. Microwaves are used to transmit and receive communications and to cook food (in microwave ovens). Radar operates with microwaves, too. Microwaves range in wavelengths from a fraction of an inch to a few inches in length.

Television and FM radio signals are transmitted on short radio wavelengths that are about 10 feet (3 m) in length. AM radio broadcasts on much longer wavelengths—they are about the size of one or two football fields.

The other way to describe a radio wave is by its frequency. This is used when dialing to a radio station. You twist the tuning dial until the frequency of the station is shown.

Frequency and wavelength are related. The wavelength multiplied by the frequency equals the speed of the wave (the speed of light). Since the speed of electromagnetic waves is constant, as the wavelength increases the frequency decreases. Long-wavelength radio waves have low frequencies; short-wavelength waves have high frequencies.

Radio Station Transmitting Antenna

BEHAVIOR
Sends radio programs out through the atmosphere so radio receivers can pick up the signals.

HABITAT
On tall towers in open fields. Towers for AM stations are typically 250 to 500 feet (75 to 150 m) tall and are usually located in groups with wires stretched between them. Collectively they can transmit the radio signal farther. AM signals (operating at much lower frequency than FM signals) can bounce off the lower atmosphere and be received far beyond the line of sight of their antennas.

FM towers are often higher—unlike AM towers, they have to be tall enough to have a "line of sight" with all of their receiving radios or their signals will be prevented from getting to some of the radios.

HOW IT WORKS
A radio station amplifies its signal (which transmits voices or music), shifts it to a higher frequency, and sends it to the station's antenna. The antenna transforms the electrical signal into an electromagnetic wave that travels at the speed of light.

UNIQUE CHARACTERISTICS
The antenna is attached to the side or the top of the tower. Look for a wire antenna or several wire antennas sticking up from the tower. The tower pictured here supports many antennas including radio station transmitting antennas and microwave dishes.

Television Antenna

BEHAVIOR
It picks up the electromagnetic signals broadcast by a television station and converts them into electrical signals that the television can interpret to show a program.

HABITAT
Tops of houses and apartment buildings. The higher the antenna is, the more likely it is to capture a strong signal.

HOW IT WORKS
This antenna has several arms that make it better able to capture various television signals. Each arm is a different length and captures a different frequency, or television channel. For example, UHF (ultra-high frequency) channels (those above channel 13) use high-frequency waves that are best captured by short arms.

UNIQUE CHARACTERISTICS
An antenna needs to be aimed toward the television stations' broadcast antennas. If the broadcast antennas are located near each other, a fixed receiving antenna works well. However, if the stations are widely separated, home antennas may need to move to pick up the signals well. To accomplish this, a *rotator* may be installed on the antenna. A rotator is a geared motor that turns the antenna to face different broadcast antennas. Look for a box with wires coming out of it at the base of an antenna that's attached to a house. Inside the house, probably on top of the television set, there is a box with a dial that the owner can use to rotate the antenna.

Television Satellite Dish Antenna

BEHAVIOR
Receives electromagnetic signals that contain television programs from satellites. National television networks and cable broadcast channels transmit programs to satellites using powerful transmitters and large satellite dish antennas. Local television stations and cable companies have several large satellite dishes to receive these network and cable channel broadcasts from the satellites. Once the broadcasts are received by the station they are sent by cable, or retransmitted, to your home television set.

HABITAT
Television stations have several large satellite dishes; many homes have smaller, 18-inch- to 36-inch-wide (46- to 90-cm-wide) dishes to pick up satellite signals.

HOW IT WORKS
Broadcast satellites are launched into geosynchronous orbit 22,300 miles above the equator. Geosynchronous means that they stay in sync with the earth; that is, they stay in the same location relative to the earth. A television satellite dish is aimed toward a satellite so it can pick up the signal.

Anything (trees or buildings) between the satellite and the television antenna can interfere with or weaken the signal. For this reason, antennas are set up where they have a clear view of the satellite.

Networks broadcast or uplink television transmissions to a satellite. Some providers encrypt, or scramble, their signals so people who haven't paid for their service can't use it.

The satellite amplifies the signal and sends it back to Earth at a frequency that home receivers (or local television stations) are set to.

The bowl-shaped dish of the home antenna collects and focuses the weak signal onto the actual antenna, which is located in the small cylinder held above the dish.

UNIQUE CHARACTERISTICS

Moss doesn't always grow on the north sides of trees, but satellite dishes in the Northern Hemisphere are always pointed toward the south. However, they don't point directly south. There isn't enough room in space to put all the satellites directly south of you. Some satellites may be found to the east or west along the equator, but all are pretty much in line with it. So you can tell rough directions by a seeing what direction television satellite antenna point.

INTERESTING FACTS

No matter how your television receives its signal—directly from a satellite, from a cable, or from a local broadcast—the signal probably traveled by satellite at some time. Cable companies and local television stations have large antennas (called downlinks) to receive programs from sport events occurring in distant locations or corporate uplink stations. If the program you're watching originated outside your region, it probably was beamed into space and back before getting to your television.

They're hard to see, but they're up there. The satellites that provide direct broadcast signals to homes are about 22 feet (6.5 m) across and about 85 feet (26 m) long, including their antennas and solar panels. Each weighs about as much as a car. The solar panels provide the power the satellites need to amplify the signals and rebroadcast them toward Earth.

Want to look at a satellite? To find out when one will be flying by your area, visit the Heavens-Above Web site at www.heavens-above.com. By typing in your location you can find out what satellites will be passing by you at different times. To see them you'll need to be in a dark location—not in the middle of a big, brightly lit city. The best viewing will be on nights when the moon is new (when the moon is visible during daylight hours, not at night). Check the weather page of a local newspaper to find the phases of the moon.

Satellite Broadcast (Uplink) Antenna

BEHAVIOR
Broadcasts many television programs to a satellite located above the equator. The satellite rebroadcasts the signals and beams them down to homes.

HABITAT
Because there are only a handful of companies that offer direct broadcast satellite service, there are only a few places you will see this huge antenna. DIRECTV's uplink antennas are in Castle Rock, Colorado. EchoStar has its uplinks in Cheyenne, Wyoming. USSB is in Oakdale, Minnesota. AlphaStar's uplink is in Oxford, Connecticut.

A mobile uplink is a truck that carries a large uplink antenna and a transmitter. These are used to provide satellite uplinks for special events and sporting events.

HOW IT WORKS
A television program may be received by a broadcast station in one of three ways. It can come in by satellite, over optical fiber cables, or as videotape. To get programs to local stations by satellite, they have to be sent up to the satellites by either a mobile uplink truck or a fixed uplink station.

UNIQUE CHARACTERISTICS
Look for a really large dish antenna—it measures about 30 to 40 feet (9 to 12 m) across.

Radio Telescope

BEHAVIOR
Collects faint radio signals from outer space. Researchers search for sources of radio waves primarily to detect stars, but they also search for them in their quest to identify intelligent life on other planets.

HABITAT
Radio astronomy observatories. There aren't many of them; a list of U.S.-operated observatories is available at www.nas.edu/bpa1.

HOW IT WORKS
Astronomers point these motorized telescopes toward an area of the sky they want to study. Sensors indicate when a telescope is in position.

Radio waves reflect off the large bowl of the telescope (just as light reflects off a mirror) onto the can (feed horn) in the center. The shape of the antenna makes all the signals bouncing off different parts of the antenna arrive at the feed horn at the same time. The signals are picked up inside the can and travel by wires to computers, where they are analyzed and recorded.

INTERESTING FACTS
A radio telescope can detect signals much weaker than an optical telescope can, so astronomers can explore much farther into space using radio telescopes.

Cell Phone Tower

BEHAVIOR

Receives and transmits cell phone calls made in the immediate vicinity of the tower.

HABITAT

They're everywhere, or so it seems. You often see these towers, with their three-sided antennas, beside major roads. Also, look on the top of buildings. Since many people don't like the sight of the towers, telephone companies are placing the three antennas on the sides of buildings. They're also found on tops of towers that blend in with trees and even inside church steeples.

HOW IT WORKS

Each cell tower sends and receives telephone messages made within the area that surrounds it. The three boxes that make up the cell tower antenna each contain one transmitter and two receivers. The boxes are tall, thin rectangles mounted adjacent to each other.

UNIQUE CHARACTERISTICS

On top of the tower you may see another vertical antenna. This antenna keeps in contact with each of the cell phones in the area. If you have a cell phone you'll notice that every few seconds it sends a beep (and shows this with a blinking light), or radio transmission, to the vertical antenna on the closest cell site. Computers keep track of where each cell phone is so they can route calls to the phone.

To save money, one tower may support two or three sets of cell phone antennas or other types of antennas. Look to see how many sets of antennas are on the towers near you.

Look for a small building at the base of the cell telephone tower.

Cell radio equipment provides coverage for an area that's usually 2 to 10 miles (3 to 16 km) in radius. When you turn on a cell phone, it searches for the strongest signal coming from the antenna on a cell tower that it can find. When it figures out which signal is strongest (it usually identifies signals from several different cell towers at the same time) it locks onto it.

Once locked onto a cell tower, the mobile phone sends a signal to identify itself. The cell tower transmits this signal either through a microwave radio link or by cable to a mobile telephone switching office (MTSO). An MTSO isn't an actual office. It's a small building that you may see at the base of a cell tower. The MTSO searches for telephone calls that are being sent to your phone. If it finds one, it sends an alert message for your phone to all the cell sites it controls.

Each cell site sends a message to your phone. Your phone (you still don't know anyone is trying to call you) sends a message back that it has received the message and it is ready to receive a call. The MTSO then assigns radio channels and the best cell site to use. Your telephone tunes to the channels assigned by the MTSO. Then the MTSO sends a signal to ring your phone (finally!).

After the MTSO confirms that your phone rang, it sends a signal (the sound of a phone ringing) to the person calling. (Ever notice how quickly people seem to answer a telephone call? Their phone rings before you hear the ringing, so they get a jump start.)

As you move during a phone conversation, the MTSO figures out which cell should serve your phone, based on the strength of the radio signal from your phone. If you move away from one cell and closer to another, the MTSO will direct your call to the closer cell tower and you won't notice any changes while you're talking.

Although cell telephone systems operate via radio waves, the phones don't act like radios. If you're talking on a radio (such as a CB radio), no one else can talk at the same time. When you've finished talking, you have to signal the other person that you're done by saying "over" or something else. But you don't have to do that with cellular telephones.

When using a cell phone you're using two radio channels, not one. One carries your voice to the cell tower and the other carries the other person's voice to your phone. The name for this is *duplex* service. CB radio is an example of *simplex* service.

From the MTSO the telephone signal can be sent directly to another cell phone or it can be transmitted by copper wires, optical fibers, or microwave antennas to a landline (wired) central office.

This houses electronics that send the signals and telephone conversations to a switching center. The communications go out over regular telephone lines or via a microwave system (look for a microwave dish).

If you are close to the tower, look for a set of wires that ground the tower in case of a lightning strike.

INTERESTING FACTS

The car phone was invented in 1946, but it wasn't a cellular phone. It operated like the radio on a ship, not like a telephone. Radio systems have one antenna that broadcasts the signal over a large area. Cellular systems have many small cells, each with its own antenna. While driving along a road, you pass from one cell to the next.

Switching from one cell to another and keeping track of the hundreds or thousands of cell phones in an area requires modern computers. The first cellular system was installed in Japan in 1979; the second system was installed a few months later in Chicago.

Can you guess what it costs to build a cell site (which includes a building, electronics, and a tower)? The cost is about $250,000. As you travel down the highway, count the number of cell towers you see. There's a lot of money invested in this mobile communications system.

Doppler Radar

BEHAVIOR
Meteorologists use Doppler radar to identify and track the movements and structures of storms.

HABITAT
Airports and National Weather Service stations operate Doppler radar, as do professional and amateur weather forecasters.

HOW IT WORKS
Doppler radar sends radar signals over an area and detects the movement of particles that reflect off the radar. Movement causes changes in the frequency of the reflected radar signal. The greater the change in frequency, the faster the movement of the particles. Dangerous storms have high wind speeds that cause many particles to move quickly, so they give good return signals on Doppler radar. The value of this system is that it allows meteorologists to predict the severity of storms and in what direction they are moving.

Citizen's Band (CB) Antenna

BEHAVIOR
Transmits and receives radio signals at the frequencies used by citizen's band (CB) radio.

HABITAT
Roofs and bumpers of cars and trucks throughout the country. Small, removable antennas are attached to the roofs of cars with strong magnets. Longer "whip" antennas are bolted to vehicles' bumpers.

HOW IT WORKS
Two or more people with CB transceivers (a transmitter and a receiver built into one unit) can talk to each other over one of 40 frequency channels. One channel is established as a "calling channel" for people to make contact on. Once contact is made, both parties agree to switch to another channel that has less traffic.

In the United States, Channel 9 is used exclusively for emergency communications. Channel 19 is the trucker's channel (not because any agency said it had to be, but that's the channel truckers use to talk to one another). Unlike telephone conversations, CB conversations are open to anyone who wants to listen in. CBs typically operate over a range of about 5 miles (8 km).

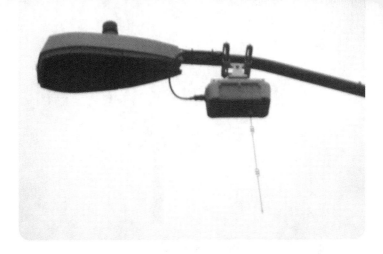

Wireless Internet Transmitter/Receiver

BEHAVIOR
Allows up to 200 computers in a neighborhood to connect to the Internet without using telephone wires or cable wires.

HABITAT
The transmitter/receiver is hung from a light pole. Because it requires electric power to operate, you will see a power cable going from the transmitter/receiver into the light pole to connect to the electric lines. You will also see an antenna hanging down from the unit. Currently this service is found only in cities where enough people in a small area want wireless Internet service.

HOW IT WORKS
A smaller transmitter/receiver is attached to the side of a home and connects to a computer inside the house. This transmitter/receiver exchanges data with the device you see hanging from the light pole. This device sends the signals to a facility that transmits the signals to optical fibers, eventually to link to the Internet.

Antenna for Satellite Internet Service

BEHAVIOR
Sends and receives radio signals between a home computer and a satellite. The satellite sends the signals to a ground station that is connected to the Internet.

HABITAT
This is a new but growing technology that is offered in dozens of countries. It is most applicable in areas that aren't well served by ground-based, high-speed Internet coverage.

HOW IT WORKS
First-generation systems required users to send signals over a telephone line and receive downloads from a satellite. Newer systems directly upload to and download from a geosynchronous satellite.

UNIQUE CHARACTERISTICS
Look for two-foot by three-foot (60- to 90-cm) antennas on the roofs of houses. (Larger antennas are required in some areas.) Like all antennas serviced by geosynchronous satellites (satellites 22,300 miles above the equator, whose positions stay fixed relative to Earth), these antennas face toward the south.

Auto Satellite Radio Antenna

Receives radio signals from one of two satellite systems so you can listen, from anywhere in the country, to one of two radio stations that currently use this system.

The antenna is usually mounted on the rear windshield, roof, or trunk of a vehicle (but it can also be used in a home or boat). The antenna is about 10 inches (25 cm) long and is angled toward the rear of the car so it forms the outline of a shark fin. It is much shorter than a typical radio antenna on a car.

Two companies (XM Satellite Radio and Sirius Satellite Radio) currently provide satellite radio. Each has its own radio stations that produce programs. The programs are digitally compressed and uplinked to satellites that broadcast the signals back to Earth.

XM Satellite Radio uses two geosynchronous satellites. These are located above the equator on opposite sides of the United States. Sirius has three satellites that aren't stationary—they revolve around the earth. One satellite is always broadcasting to the United States, while the others broadcast to other parts of the world.

Each company broadcasts about 100 channels of music, talk, and other types of programs. To use the system, a listener purchases and installs the radio and antenna and pays a subscription fee.

XM Satellite Radio calls its two satellites "Rock" and "Roll."

Antenna Field

BEHAVIOR
Provides, as a result of its height, a great location for radio communication antennas—and provides a good income for the location's owner.

HABITAT
Typically the tallest building or one of the tallest buildings in a city holds a collection of antennas. Look at the tops of buildings to see which is loaded with antennas.

HOW IT WORKS
Public agencies and private companies contract with the building's owner to put their antennas on the building's roof. Police, fire, and telephone antennas are commonly found on such roofs. The building's owner can make a lot of money renting space on the roof. The agencies and companies that have their antennas there save money by not having to build tall towers to hold up their antennas.

IN THE AIR AND NEAR AIRPORTS

THEY'RE EVERYWHERE! Anytime and anywhere you look up you likely will see a flying machine, lights, or contrails. Things get more interesting as you approach or step inside an airport.

Airports feature many more types of roadside technology than just radar, radio antennas, landing lights, and the aerial hubbub of air traffic. Once you get near an airport, you can really start to see the intricate and mighty gizmos that combine to make air transportation. Strange-looking trucks push and pull airplanes around and provide service to them, and the planes themselves are the most techno-logically advanced equipment on the planet. Most of their wondrous technology is hidden beneath the aluminum sheathing, but a few devices stick out where you can see them.

VOR Station

BEHAVIOR
Sends out high-frequency radio signals that help pilots navigate.

HABITAT
You can find a VOR station on the ground every 50 miles or so along air routes throughout the country. Most often you see them near airports.

HOW IT WORKS
The VOR antenna is the bowling pin-shaped structure on top of these stations. VOR stands for VHF Omnidirectional Range (VHF refers to "very high frequency").

VORs transmit a radio signal. Each VOR uses a different frequency so pilots can tune in on a frequency to listen for a particular VOR. Pilots can find the frequency of a VOR station by looking it up on a navigation map. They dial in the VOR transmitting frequency via a special radio receiver that shows them the direction to the station. Pilots can fly across the country from one VOR station to another by following the signals from one to the next.

OK, it's a bit more complex than that. A pilot dials in the angle at which they want to approach the VOR station. A needle on the pilot's radio shows what direction the plane needs to fly to stay on track.

The VOR transmits two signals at once. One signal travels out in all directions. The second travels outward in a straight line as it rotates in a circle. The first signal is similar to ripples on a pond after you've chucked a stone into it. The second signal is similar to the beam of light emitted from a lighthouse as it rotates. An airplane's receiver measures the difference in the time it takes to receive the two signals. The time difference indicates the direction to the VOR station.

UNIQUE CHARACTERISTICS
Check out an air navigation map and you will see the VOR stations marked on it. They are the large circles shown with lines radiating from them. Your library might have air navigation maps; certainly there are some at the civil air terminal of any airport.

Deicing Boot

BEHAVIOR
Removes ice from the wings of airplanes.

HABITAT
Look on the leading edges of the wings and tails of smaller commercial airplanes.

HOW IT WORKS
The boot is made of rubber. Inside is a series of tubes through which air can be pumped. A device inflates the tubes, causing the rubber to expand, and then sucks the air out, causing the rubber to contract. The rapid change in the size of the rubber boot causes ice to break and fall off.

UNIQUE CHARACTERISTICS
Look for the black boot over the front of the wing or tail.

Pitot Tube

BEHAVIOR

A pitot (PEA-toe) tube measures the speed of an airplane. When a pilot announces that the airplane is traveling 534 miles per hour through the air, he or she may be reading an instrument connected to the pitot tube.

HABITAT

The tube is found on the side of an airplane, often below the cockpit. It's about 10 inches (25 cm) long and 1 inch (2.5 cm) wide.

HOW IT WORKS

A pitot tube is actually two tubes in one. It has a center opening that connects to one side of a *pressure transducer* (an instrument that measures pressure). The holes in the sides of the pitot tube connect to the other side of the pressure transducer. The difference in pressure between the two is related to the speed of the pitot tube as it travels through the air.

UNIQUE CHARACTERISTICS

If you can get close enough to examine a pitot tube, notice that there are several holes near the end of the tube and a hole in the center of the tube. The tube is pointed so that the center hole faces into the direction of travel. As the plane flies, air flows into the center hole, causing a change in pressure that is related to the plane's speed.

Vortex Generator

BEHAVIOR
Creates vortices (whirling streams) in the air that flow over the wing of an airplane as it travels through the air.

HABITAT
Vortex generators are used on many, but not all, commercial aircraft. Look on the forward part of the plane's wings, about halfway on the wings between the fuselage (the aircraft body) and the wings' tips.

HOW IT WORKS
The generator causes passing air to swirl. The swirling disturbances help keep the air in contact with the wing, which reduces the drag.

UNIQUE CHARACTERISTICS
Look for a row of small metal tabs sticking up from the top surface of the wing.

Ground Power Unit (GPU)

BEHAVIOR
Provides electrical power and air conditioning for airplanes while they are on the ground.

HABITAT
You can find these units at most airports. Larger airports provide power and air conditioning from connections found in the concrete pavement beneath the airplanes. Watch as ground crews make hose connections to a plane.

HOW IT WORKS
The GPU has a diesel engine inside that powers an electrical generator and an air conditioner.

UNIQUE CHARACTERISTICS
Planes carry their own auxiliary power units, or APUs, to provide air conditioning to aircraft. On the ground, however, ground crews will pull over a GPU, which is much larger and stronger, to provide air conditioning.

The hoses that ground crews connect to planes are color coded. Yellow hoses provide air conditioning, either from a GPU or from the ground (some airports pipe conditioned air out to airplanes). Small blue hoses provide water for the lavatories. Larger, dark tubes called "biffy" tubes carry lavatory waste out of the airplane.

NEAR NAVIGABLE WATERS

NAVIGABLE WATERS ARE WATERWAYS that are deep enough and wide enough for a ship to travel through them. If they're large enough to accommodate ships, rivers and bays have "aids to navigation." These are markers that mariners can use to find their positions and to avoid rocks, reefs, and other obstructions.

Channel Marker Buoy

BEHAVIOR

Shows mariners where the boundaries of a channel (the deepest part of a river or other waterway) are. The depth of the water between the buoys and the waterway's shores may be too shallow for a boat or ship.

It's a bad day for a mariner who runs a boat or ship aground. The ship may not be able to get back to deep water, and it may be damaged. For this reason, mariners use the buoys as guides to stick to the channels.

HABITAT

Channel marker buoys are used in rivers and bays, and in the ocean offshore of harbors. (The buoys pictured here are on shore, next to a maritime museum.)

HOW IT WORKS

A buoy is a floating aid to navigation. The color of the marker indicates the direction in which boats and ships should be steered to stay in the channel. When coming in from the sea, mariners keep the red markers on their right side and the green are on their left. Sailors remember this as "the three Rs of navigation": red, right, returning. Returning means coming back from a trip on the ocean.

INTERESTING FACTS

Floating red markers are called nuns. The top of a nun is conical in shape. These buoys are marked with even numbers. Floating green markers are called cans. They are square or cylindrical in shape, and they're marked with odd numbers.

Lighted Bell Buoy

BEHAVIOR
Guides mariners along channels or away from dangerous shallows via lights and bells (or some other type of audible warning system).

HABITAT
In waterways near shoals (shallows) that ships need to avoid.

HOW IT WORKS
This type of buoy features lights and a bell and hammers as aids to navigation. As waves from an approaching ship rock the buoy, one or more of four hammers strikes the bell. Some buoys also have foghorns. Today, solar cells provide power for the lights and horns of these markers. The electric power generated by the solar cells is stored in a battery to power these devices at night.

During the day, mariners can usually identify buoys by their numbers, shapes, and colors. However, at night or in fog, buoys may be hard to spot. This is why so many buoys have lights, bells, gongs, electric-powered horns, or wave-powered whistles. Mariners can determine which buoy they're looking at by observing its flashing light pattern (how long the light is on and off). Nuns have red lights and cans have green lights.

UNIQUE CHARACTERISTICS
The first buoy that a ship encounters as it comes from the sea into a port is marked with the number one. The numbers increase farther up the channel, away from the sea.

At night, look for flashing lights on the buoys. Each buoy in a harbor has a different sequence of flashes so mariners can tell the markers apart. Navigational charts show mariners the light pattern of each lighted buoy.

Range Marker

BEHAVIOR
Helps navigators find their way along narrow channels.

HABITAT
Range markers are used along rivers that have ship traffic. They are found onshore or in shallow water, and they are usually on tall, wooden poles.

HOW IT WORKS
Range markers come in pairs, one behind the other, usually mounted on two poles. They help navigators determine the location of the center of the channel. To position a boat or ship in the center of the channel, the helmsman steers the vessel so that from it, the front and rear markers are aligned, one behind the other. Most have a vertical line painted in the center. When the two center lines match up, the ship is in the channel.

A ship can navigate up a channel by following one set of range markers after another. Nautical charts show where to find the range markers and indicate where a ship should turn to catch the next one.

UNIQUE CHARACTERISTICS
Range markers make great nesting spots for ospreys and other marine birds. Look for a huge nest, made of branches, on the tops of markers or on the tops of the posts supporting the markers.

Lighthouse

BEHAVIOR
Indicates a prominent position to sailors. A lighthouse's color and light beam allow sailors to identify different lighthouses and to refer to charts to determine their location.

The taller a light is, the farther from shore the light can be seen. Lighthouses are built as tall as necessary to ensure that sailors can see their lights before getting close to dangerous areas such as shallow reefs.

Some lighthouses also have sound-making devices and radio beacons so sailors can find them in fog.

HABITAT
Along shorelines and rock outcroppings.

HOW IT WORKS
Each lighthouse has a unique marking that allows sailors to identify it during daylight hours. For night identification, lighthouses have different-colored lights and different patterns of flashing lights. Navigational charts show the flashing patterns. Once sailors determine which light they're looking at, they measure the compass direction of the light from their ship. They draw a line with that angle from the position of light on the nautical chart. Their ship is somewhere on that line. Having bearings to two or more lights allows them to draw two or more lines. The ship is located where the lines intersect on the chart.

Go to a library, map store, or marine supply store to look at nautical charts. Ask to see the key for the symbols found on the charts so you can figure out what they represent. Looking at a chart, find a light and look at the numbers beside it to see the length of time between its flashes. If you live near the lighthouse, check out its light at night. See if you can identify the lighthouse by its light pattern.

Lightship

BEHAVIOR
Aided mariners by beaming powerful lights at night, usually at the mouth of a river or harbor.

HABITAT
Not at sea. You will find the last lightships at nautical museums. When they were in use, lightships marked the openings to harbors or rivers and indicated the position of dangerous shoals. The last lightship, the Nantucket Shoals Light, was replaced in 1983 by a *Large Navigational Buoy* (see page 151).

HOW IT WORKS
The lightships were moored in position and remained in place for years, until they needed to go to dry docks for maintenance or repairs. A small crew of coastguardsmen lived onboard and operated each ship, keeping the lights working. The crews were exchanged every week or two.

UNIQUE CHARACTERISTICS
Lightships have a distinct shape and coloration that makes them easy to distinguish from other ships that may be displayed at a nautical museum. They are broad in the beam, are short fore and aft, and feature their station names written in big white letters on each side of their hulls. The hulls are painted red. Perched atop their tall masts are one or more lights.

INTERESTING FACTS
At one time the there were 56 working lightships throughout the United States. In the 1970s and 1980s *Large Navigational Buoy*s (see page 151) replaced them.

Large Navigational Buoy

BEHAVIOR

The Large Navigational Buoy (LNB) replaced the *lightship* (see page 150) and was itself phased out in the 1990s. The buoys were stationed at the mouths of rivers or harbors to guide ships coming in. These buoys were huge. Standing 60 feet (18 m) tall, they were so big that each had two diesel motors inside that power electrical generators to provide electricity for the lights.

The coast guard has replaced LNBs with smaller buoys that are powered by solar cells. In addition to the navigational lights, these buoys have sound signals and radio beacons to help ships find them.

HABITAT

LNBs, like the lightships they replaced, are now found only at maritime museums. The LNB buoy shown in this photo was used at the mouth of the Columbia River. It replaced the Columbia River lightship in 1979 and it was replaced in 1993. Refueling and repairing these huge buoys was difficult in rough waters, so the coast guard replaced them.

HOW IT WORKS

The buoy has its own electrical generator to power its navigational lights and data recording instruments. It could be outfitted with instruments to measure wind, waves, temperature, precipitation, and ocean currents.

Ship Radar and Communication Antenna

BEHAVIOR
Allows mariners to send and receive electromagnetic signals.

HABITAT
The upper levels of ships and boats.

HOW IT WORKS
Refer to the photograph shown here. This photograph shows a U.S. coast guard cutter (a type of ship).

The white loop antenna in the foreground is for high-frequency radio transmissions and e-mail. As backup for this antenna, the cutter also has small whip antennas (wires sticking straight up), as shown in the upper part of the photo.

The two-loop antenna on top of the cutter is the antenna for a radio direction finder. This device allows its operator to locate a strong radio signal and find the direction to the radio transmitting the signal. In this way, the radio direction finder can hone in on a ship's distress signal, or it can be used to help navigate a ship by finding the direction to a radio station at a known location on land.

The tall whip antennas are for marine radio communications. The white domes house radar. The white bars are navigational radar. They rotate around about once per second, sending out a signal that reflects off other ships or land. The reflected signal appears on a screen on the ship's bridge and shows the distance and positions of ships and points of land.

UNIQUE CHARACTERISTICS
Although different ships may have different collections of antennas, the distinctive shapes, sizes, and functions of them are the same as those discussed here.

Super Post-Panamax Crane

BEHAVIOR

This crane is designed to unload container ships that are too big to pass through the Panama Canal. A Panamax ship is one that is the maximum size that can navigate the locks. Post-Panamax ships are too big to get through. These super large ships use these super large cranes to off-load and on-load containers. It lifts containers from the deck or inside the hull of a cargo container ship and moves them to waiting trucks with trailers. As each container is set on a trailer, it is attached to the trailer. Then the truck driver drives away and another truck pulls into position.

HABITAT

This crane can be found in ports around the world.

HOW IT WORKS

Products are put into large containers before they are shipped. This allows shipping companies to load and unload shipments much more quickly and with less chance of theft or breakage. Before containers were used, cargo was carried in bulk, which meant that longshoremen had to load individual packages onto a pallet and have a crane operator lift the pallet away. Now, cargo is packed and locked in containers and goes directly from the ship to the truck without anyone having to touch the individual products inside the containers. Containers cut the time needed to load and unload ships, which saves money.

When you're at or near a port, watch how quickly cargo containers are moved off a ship.

Container Ship

BEHAVIOR
Transports hundreds of containers of cargo on its deck and inside its hull.

HABITAT
Container ships have replaced most of the traditional cargo ships everywhere in the world. You can see them in large ports, in harbors, and on the high seas.

HOW IT WORKS
Manufacturers pack, lock shut, and seal containers and deliver them to the dock via trailer trucks. Giant cranes lift the containers from the trailer and load them on or in a waiting ship. At the receiving port, the containers are loaded directly onto trailers or rail cars and are hauled to their destination.

INTERESTING FACTS
In order for this system to work, the containers must all be the same size. Containers are either 20 feet (6 m) or 40 feet (12 m) long, a little over 7 ½ feet (2.3 m) wide and 8 feet (2.4 m) tall. They are referred to as 20-foot equivalent units, or TEUs. Container ships can be enormous. Some are big enough to carry over 1,000 TEUs. Think of 1,000 truck trailers stacked in huge piles on a ship—that gives you an idea of how big a container ship is. Some ship builders now construct container ships that carry 8,000 containers.

Log Carrier

BEHAVIOR
Log carriers transport unmilled logs from where they are harvested to lumber mills.

HABITAT
Log carriers are prevalent in the waters of the Pacific Northwest and British Columbia.

HOW IT WORKS
Log-carrying vessels come in a variety of sizes and carry different volumes of cargo. A typical ship measures 560 feet (170 m) in length. It can carry approximately 23,000 logs in its cargo hatches and on its deck.

To put that number of logs into perspective, think of the number of acres of land that need to be cleared to fill the ship. One tree may yield three or four 32-foot-long (10-meter-long) logs. Depending on how well managed the forest lands are, there might be 200 trees on each acre. Thus, one ship carries the logs made from 30 to 35 acres of forest trees.

Log carriers have multiple cranes onboard, which allow the ship's cargo to be loaded and unloaded without needing cranes on the dock.

Bulk Carrier

BEHAVIOR
Transports unprocessed agricultural products.

HABITAT
Bulk carriers are a common sight at ports, especially those that serve agricultural exports.

HOW IT WORKS
Agricultural products are vacuum pumped or dropped from grain elevators (large storage buildings) into the holds (open cargo areas) of a ship. At the discharging port, giant vacuums suck out the cargo and feed it into rail cars for delivery to food processing plants. The bulk carrier pictured here is called the *Ocean Behavior*. It carries beet pellets, soy meal, and corn gluten meal.

Cable-Laying Ship

BEHAVIOR
Lays optical fiber or conventional wire cables, used in communications technologies, on the seafloor.

HABITAT
Predominantly in busy ports, where ships will take on supplies between jobs.

HOW IT WORKS
Cable is rolled off either the bow or the stern. It's easy to determine that the ship pictured here lays cable off its stern, since all the cranes and machinery are visible on the stern. The stern is where the large open deck is, which is used by the workers as they roll out the cable. Ships that lay cable from their bows have a large wheel or pulley on the bow for the cable to roll over.

To protect the cable, the ship tows a plow to dig a trench in the ocean bottom. The cable is then laid in the trench. The trench becomes filled with sediment (sand and mud), burying the cable about six feet (2 m) under the ocean's bottom.

An optical fiber cable contains more than just optical fibers. The signals traveling through each fiber have to be amplified, so the cable has a repeater spliced into it every 30 miles (48 km) or so.

UNIQUE CHARACTERISTICS
As you look at a ship, figure out which end is where the work happens. Whether the ship catches fish or lays cable, the crew needs a flat place to stand, and they need equipment to move heavy loads onto the ship and into the sea. Then ask yourself what job could be done in the space available and with the machinery you see. After you've made a guess, call the port authority and ask them what ships are in port to see if your guess is right.

Floating Dry Dock

It is the equivalent of a hydraulic lift in a gas station, except that the floating dry dock goes to the ship. The ship doesn't have to come to it.

HABITAT
Many ports have floating dry docks as well as fixed dry docks. To find one, look along the shores of the industrial part of a port for a large structure in the shape of the letter "U" that has open ends.

HOW IT WORKS
A floating dry dock either propels itself or is towed by a tug to a ship that needs repairs. Water is let into holding tanks inside the dry dock, causing it to slowly sink. When the water inside the dry dock (it's not so dry now, is it?) is deep enough to accommodate the ship, the ship is pulled into the dock. Divers then set huge blocks under the ship to support it. When the ship is lined up on top of the blocks, the water in the dry dock tanks is blown out with air pressure. As air replaces water in the tanks, the dry dock rises, lifting the ship. Once the ship is out of the water, engineers can inspect the hull and workers can repair damage. It takes an hour or two for a floating dry dock to lift a ship out of the water.

Ferry

BEHAVIOR
Carries people, cars, and trucks over water.

HABITAT
Ferries operate in cities that contain rivers or harbors and in rural areas where roads cross rivers. In most places, bridges have replaced ferries. However, in some places the cost of building a bridge would be much higher than is the cost of operating a ferry.

HOW IT WORKS
The typical ferry is two-ended. That means either end of the ship can dock close to shore. Picture a ferry at a terminal. Cars, all heading in one direction, drive onto it. It is far easier and safer to have the cars continue to drive forward to disembark (go ashore) once the ferry reaches its destination. Because the ferry has to be able to let cars and trucks on and off from either end, most ferries have two pilothouses (navigational rooms) and two sets of propellers and rudders.

UNIQUE CHARACTERISTICS
When you're approaching a major ferry terminal on land, a fleet of rushing cars will tell you that a ferry has landed.

Oceanographic Research Ship

BEHAVIOR
It takes oceanographers to places where they conduct experiments on the ocean, the animals that live in it, or the rocks and sediments under it.

HABITAT
Research vessels can be found in dozens of ports in the United States. Most research ships are affiliated with either the federal government or with colleges and universities, and they are homeported near these organizations. The ship pictured here is Oregon State University's R/V (research vessel) *Wecoma*.

HOW IT WORKS
Researchers and students make up about half the crew on research vessels. The other half consists of professional sailors who operate the ship.

UNIQUE CHARACTERISTICS
Most research ships have a crane for hauling nets, current meters, or other devices out of the water. Usually the largest cranes are located near the stern of the ship. When a ship is conducting research it flies a symbol to notify other ships to stay away. The symbol is a ball below a diamond, which is below another ball. All three shapes are colored black.

INTERESTING FACTS
Some research ships give tours when they are in port. Check with the port authority or the organization that owns the ship to request a tour.

Icebreaker

BEHAVIOR

This ship isn't used to help start parties. Instead, it is designed to travel through polar seas and the Great Lakes to break through seasonal sea ice. It can carry supplies for researchers, and it can open leads in ice for other ships to follow. In addition, scientists and ship crews use these ships to perform polar research and to conduct search-and-rescue missions in areas of high latitudes.

HABITAT

Unless you live in Alaska, you're most likely to see a U.S. icebreaker in its home port of Seattle, Washington. The U.S. coast guard also operates one icebreaker in the Great Lakes. To see images of icebreakers, both historic and current, go to the U.S. coast guard site at www.uscg.mil/hq/g-cp/history/Icebreaker_Photo_Index_1.html.

HOW IT WORKS

An icebreaker has a strong hull and engine to power it through the ice. But that alone won't break ice. The ship has an oddly shaped bow. It curves under the ship, which allows the ship to slide up and over ice. Then the weight of the ship breaks through the ice, allowing the ship to move forward. So, rather than breaking the ice by battering it, the icebreaker sits on top of the ice to break it.

The *Polar Sea* and the *Polar Star*, the U.S. coast guard's polar icebreakers, are the most powerful nonnuclear icebreakers in the world. They are nearly 400 feet (120 m) long and have a skin made of $1^3/_4$-inch-thick (4.4-cm-thick) steel. They can break through ice as thick as six feet (1.8 m) while moving at about three and a half miles (5.6 km) per hour.

Plimsoll Mark

BEHAVIOR
A Plimsoll mark is load line of a ship. It shows a ship's *draft*, or how deep in the water the ship is sitting at any given time. If the ship takes on so much cargo that the Plimsoll mark is submerged, it's a sign that the ship is overloaded and that it could be in danger of capsizing.

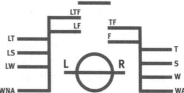

HABITAT
The starboard side (the right side, when facing the bow) of the hull of a ship.

HOW IT WORKS
As a ship takes on cargo, it sinks lower in the water. A ship always sits higher in seawater than in freshwater, since saltwater is denser (it has a greater mass per volume than does freshwater due to the salt in seawater). In addition, a ship floats higher in the water during the winter than it does during the summer, because colder water is denser than warm water. For these reasons, a Plimsoll mark is not just a single line, but a series of lines.

UNIQUE CHARACTERISTICS
Look at the illustration of a Plimsoll mark shown above. The large "L" and "R" stand for Lloyd's Register. (Lloyd's provides insurance and other services to maritime businesses.) The "S" shows the ship's load line during the summer; the "W" is the winter load line; "F" stands for freshwater; "T" stands for tropical waters. "WNA" represents the winter load line when the ship is in north Atlantic Ocean water.

INTERESTING FACTS
The mark is named for Samuel Plimsoll, a member of the British Parliament during the 1800s. He pushed for legislation requiring that ships display load lines to prevent unsafe conditions due to overloading. His work saved the lives of many sailors.

ON UTILITY POLES AND TOWERS

ATOP THE UTILITY POLES near your home are wires that bring electricity to you. The electric power system starts at power plants (see Chapter 5) and, for our purposes, ends where you plug an appliance into a wall socket.

Look up at a utility pole and you see a maze of wires and devices. This is a short road map to help you sort through what you're seeing.

The wires highest above the ground carry electricity. Usually there are three wires, as discussed below. A cross arm supports these wires and keeps them from touching each other.

Lower on the pole are cable television or broadband wires. Cable television wires can be either optical fibers or copper cable. To support these wires a steel wire is wrapped with the bundle of the copper wires or optical fibers. At each utility pole the television wires are formed into an expansion loop so that when the poles swing in a breeze the stress is placed on the steel wire and not on the delicate wires that carry television signals. Look for the loop to distinguish cable television wires from all others.

The bottom wires on the pole are telephone wires, which are made of copper.

Each set of wires connects to other equipment on or near the utility pole. Go to each section below to find out what each piece of equipment looks like and the task it performs for you.

Push Brace Pole

BEHAVIOR
Supports a utility pole.

HABITAT
On the ground, next to a utility pole.

HOW IT WORKS
A push brace pole is used wherever the sideways stress on a utility pole is excessive. For example, if all the wires the pole supports are on one side of the pole, it will need support so that it doesn't lean to that side.

Utility Pole ID

BEHAVIOR
Displays the date the pole was installed, as well as an identification number.

HABITAT
Every utility pole has one or more tags with identification numbers.

HOW IT WORKS
Imagine how many poles a utility company has to keep track of. Utility pole IDs allow a company to identify each pole and to know when it will likely need replacing or repairing.

UNIQUE CHARACTERISTICS
The tags are often metal numbers and letters. Usually they are above eye level.

Utility Pole Manual Switch

BEHAVIOR
Provides a way for workers to disconnect a power substation or a neighborhood from a city's or county's electric grid.

HABITAT
Switches are mounted on utility poles outside of electric power substations and where two or more circuits come together. The switch handle is at or near ground level, locked in position.

HOW IT WORKS
The utility pole manual switch connects to a metal pipe, which is attached to a switch at the top of the pole. The utility pole manual switch allows workers to turn off the power without having to climb the pole. Throwing the switch disconnects one part of the distribution circuit.

Grounding Wire

BEHAVIOR
Prevents people from getting hurt and equipment from getting damaged by lightning strikes and from power wires that may otherwise electrify the pole.

HABITAT
On utility poles that carry transformers; the grounding wire is connected to the transformer case. Poles that don't carry transformers can have grounding wires, but many do not.

HOW IT WORKS
The grounding wire is made of metal strands that conduct electricity. The grounding wire is a safety measure to ensure that someone touching the transformer or other parts of the pole won't get shocked. It also protects people and equipment from lightning strikes. The grounding wire provides a safe way for the electric energy to get to the ground.

UNIQUE CHARACTERISTICS
Follow the wire down the pole and into the ground. At the ground you will see a large spike that is driven into the ground. The earth is a giant conductor that can safely distribute electric charges.

Residential Drop Wires

BEHAVIOR
Three wires carry single-phase, 120-volt alternating current from the transformer on the utility pole to your electric meter. Two of the three wires carry 120 volts each; the third wire is neutral.

HABITAT
These electrical wires connect a utility pole to a home or building.

HOW IT WORKS
The two power-carrying wires are connected to opposite ends of the transformer, and the neutral wire connects to the center of the transformer. The three wires connect through the electric meter outside the home into the distribution panel, which is inside the home.

In single-phase power (the kind found in homes), the electrical currents carried in the two wires alternate at the same time. Alternating current has electrical charges moving one direction and then the other, 60 times a second. The pattern of currents is the same in the two wires in single phase.

The problem with having the currents in this type of phase is that both wires provide zero charge at the same time in the 60 cycles each second (also called 60 hertz). Heavy equipment works better if its power source doesn't drop to zero current, so many industries use three-phase power.

Electrical power is generated in three phases. Each phase runs at the same rate (60 cycles per second in the United States) and each phase has the same maximum average voltage (about 112 volts). But they start at different times. When one phase has completed a full cycle, the next phase has completed only two thirds of a cycle, and the third phase has completed only one third of the cycle. This out-of-phase feature provides heavy electric motors with a more uniform flow of power.

Distribution Transformer

BEHAVIOR
Lowers the voltage in electric wires from 7,200 volts to 240 volts.

HABITAT
Distribution transformers are hung on utility poles near the tops of the poles. In neighborhoods where the electric wires run underground, the transformer is usually located in a green metal box on the ground, although sometimes it's placed in an underground vault.

HOW IT WORKS
A distribution transformer decreases the voltage of an alternating current. Wires from a house are wrapped around one side of a hollow core made of steel or iron. Wires that carry the 7,200 volts from pole to pole are wrapped around the other side. The 7,200-volt side has 30 times the number of windings as does the house side, which reduces the voltage to one-thirtieth of 7,200 volts, or 240 volts.

Electricity applied to the 7,200 volt side creates a magnetic field. The magnetic field creates an electric current in the house side. The strength of the electric field varies directly with the number of windings.

The 240-volt side of the transformer has three connections, or *taps* (see page 194), for the wires leading to a house. The center tap is neutral; it provides zero volts. The other two taps carry alternating currents that fluctuate between +120 volts and −120 volts. They are "out of phase," meaning that when one tap has maximum positive voltage, the other has maximum negative voltage. Each of the charged lines can deliver 120 volts and combined they can deliver 240 volts, which is required for some appliances such as clothes dryers.

INTERESTING FACTS

Linemen often have to perform maintenance on these aerial transformers while they are "hot" (while electricity is flowing through them). To protect themselves from electrocution, the linemen use fiberglass "hot sticks" as tools. The fiberglass insulates them from electrical contact. The bucket truck that a lineman stands in while working on the transformer is not grounded. If it were, electricity could flow through the lineman to the bucket truck and then to the ground. This could injure or kill the lineman. The trucks are tested every month to ensure that they resist the flow of electricity.

Electrical Distribution Wires

BEHAVIOR

These three wires carry electrical power, typically at 7,200 volts, from the substation to the *distribution transformer* (see page 170).

HABITAT

Connected to utility poles at the tops of the poles. A utility pole may also carry optical fiber cable for television and copper wire for telephones, but the electrical wires are always on top.

HOW IT WORKS

The electrical power is distributed in three phases. One phase is carried by each of the three wires. If there is a fourth wire present, it is a ground wire to attract lightning away from the other wires.

Why don't birds sitting on electric wires always get shocked? As long as they aren't also touching the ground, electricity doesn't flow through them. Electricity doesn't go into a dead end. It completes a circuit or flows toward a "ground." If the birds were to touch a wire with one foot and the ground with the other foot, they might get a terrible shock. Large birds, like birds of prey, sometimes touch both a hot wire and ground at the same time and get electrocuted. Some people estimate that several tens of thousands of birds die this way every year.

Bird Deflector

BEHAVIOR
Alerts birds to the presence of guy wires and towers so they can avoid flying into them.

HABITAT
Bird deflectors are brightly colored plastic balls that are attached to guy wires and towers. Although they can be used anywhere, bird deflectors are most often used near marshy areas where waterfowl congregate.

HOW IT WORKS
This is a vision-based warning system. During the day birds can see them and the system works. However, at night they are not effective. Some people estimate that as many as 175 million birds die each year in the United States by running into wires they can't see.

INTERESTING FACTS
You may see larger deflectors on wires that stretch over rivers or valleys. These may be to warn human fliers of the presence of the wires.

Control Data Center

BEHAVIOR
Collects electric meter readings within a quarter-mile radius every 15 minutes and stores the readings before radioing them on to the electric company's data center.

HABITAT
Control data centers are housed in metal boxes that are mounted high on utility poles. You can identify one by the three antennas projecting from the metal box. The two lower antennas collect data from homes, and the upper antenna transmits the data to another center, which transmits it to the regional data center.

HOW IT WORKS

Every 15 minutes the control data center interrogates each electric meter in the neighborhood and prompts it to transmit a radio signal. The signal identifies which meter is being reported and how much electricity the customer has used since the last report. The center collects and stores this information. Every 15 minutes it radio transmits the data to a larger data center, which is also mounted on a utility pole. The larger center transmits the data to a company data center that could be as far away as 100 miles (160 km).

UNIQUE CHARACTERISTICS

Control data centers are becoming a common site in neighborhoods as electric companies are switching from having people read electric meters to collecting and sending readings by radio. See if you can find the larger, regional control data center that collects data from all the neighborhood centers in your area.

INTERESTING FACTS

The push to change old-fashioned meters to the new, radio-transmitting meters is due partly to the money saved by electric companies by not having meter readers come to your home, but it's also a result of the high cost of energy.

Utility companies now encourage people to use power when it is cheaper for the companies to provide it. For example, a company that generates power via hydroelectric dams has a steady source of power throughout the day. However, people use little electricity at night, a lot at breakfast time, and a lot at dinnertime. Utility companies often need to purchase electricity from other companies (on the "spot market") to meet their customers' demands, and that electricity is much more expensive than the electricity produced by a utility company itself. By measuring a home's electrical usage throughout the day, the company can charge people different rates that reflect the time of day that power was used. Check out your family's next electric bill to see if it shows the cost of electricity at different times of the day.

Insulator

BEHAVIOR
Protects a tower or utility pole from electricity-carrying wires that are attached to it.

HABITAT
On all poles and towers that carry electric wires.

HOW IT WORKS
Insulators are made of ceramic or other materials that have high resistance to the flow of electricity. The bigger the insulator is, or the more disks you see in the insulator, the more resistance it provides. Electric companies use more disks to carry higher voltage wires. By counting the number of disks in an insulator you can tell which wires carry higher-voltage electric power.

Regulator Bank

BEHAVIOR

Electricity is generated at three different phases, and a regulator bank balances the voltages among the three phases. Think of three waves, each running along one of three wires. The waves all travel at the same speed, but one starts before the others, then the second starts, and finally the third starts. These start times are evenly spaced, so the next wave on the first wire is spaced as far behind the wave on the third wire as it is spaced ahead of the wave on the second wire.

HABITAT

Atop utility poles in sets of three.

HOW IT WORKS

Homes tap into one of the three waves of electricity, which are called phases. Some companies use two or all three phases of the power. When one phase is used (by all of the utility company's customers) more than another, an imbalance exists between the three waves. The regulator banks—consisting of three transformers, one for each line—adjust the voltages on the three wires so they are equal.

UNIQUE CHARACTERISTICS

Above each of the three transformers is a switch. When workers need to repair the transformers they can flip the switches with a long-handled insulated pole.

It's easy to spot a regulator bank. It consists of three adjacent transformers (cylinders with wires connected to them), usually elevated above the ground between two closely-spaced utility poles. You may also see a dial in a small electric box. It shows the balance of voltages for the three lines.

Capacitor Bank

BEHAVIOR
Helps to reduce one type of resistance loss in the wires so the current can travel farther.

HABITAT
Inside power substations and on utility poles.

HOW IT WORKS
Capacitor banks reduce the overall resistance to electrical transmission. The bank includes several capacitors, and each one consists of pairs of flat conductors that are separated by a narrow gap. Input wires connect to one member of the pair and output wires connect to the other. When charges build up on the input side, they pull charges of the opposite sign on the output side. Opposite charges attract each other. Positive charges on one will attract negative charges on the other. Since the input voltage changes 60 times a second, the charges on the output side also change signs 60 times a second. Capacitors in the circuit reduce the energy losses caused by magnetic fields generated by motors powered by the electric line.

UNIQUE CHARACTERISTICS
Rather than seeing one large capacitor, a bank will hold a half dozen or more smaller capacitors.

High-Voltage Wire

BEHAVIOR
Transmits electrical current long distances.

HABITAT
High-voltage wires are strung between power plants and cities or large industrial users of electricity.

HOW IT WORKS
The metal wires let electricity pass along them. However, as electricity flows, it loses power to resistance. Over long distances of 100 miles (160 km) or more, these losses become significant. To reduce them, voltages are transformed to very high levels for transmission—hence the name "high-voltage wire."

UNIQUE CHARACTERISTICS
The height of a high-voltage wire indicates the voltage it carries. Higher voltages are required to be kept farther off the ground to prevent people from coming in contact with them. Also, the higher the voltage that is carried, the more disks you see in the insulators that hold the wire to a tower.

In almost every area of the country, three wires carry the electricity. However, you may find high-tension towers carrying two wires instead of three. In some western states electricity is transmitted as direct current (two wires) instead of alternating current (three wires).

Confused? We just said that voltages have to be very high for transmission wires, otherwise resistive losses cut the power. And we said that the voltage of direct current cannot be *transformed* or changed. So how—and why—is electricity effectively transmitted long distance via direct current? Here's how: Since direct current cannot be passed through a transformer to change its voltage, power companies transform alternating current to high voltages and then change it to direct current for transmission. At the user end of the transmission lines, the direct current is converted back to alternating current and passed through transformers to reduce its voltage. Here's why this is done: these extra steps (and expenses) are balanced out by saving the cost of one wire. A few hundred miles of high-tension wire is expensive, so if companies can save money by transmitting the electricity using two wires (direct current) instead of three (alternating current), they will. However, this process is cost effective only over very long transmission paths of several hundred miles.

INTERESTING FACTS

As you pass under high-voltage wires you can hear a crackling sound. The electricity running through the wires creates an electromagnetic field around them that can cause gases in the air to crackle. The high energy *ionizes* gas molecules—it separates molecules into electrically charged particles (ions). The molecules lose this charge when they bump into other molecules with opposite charges, and you hear the sound of this discharge.

Also, high winds blowing through the wires can make them sing (make noise). Air currents generate vortices, or little swirls of air, on the downstream side. These vortices create changes in the air pressure that we hear as sound.

In the early days of building the U.S. electrical power system there was a debate between people (such as Thomas Edison) who thought power should be distributed as direct current and those (such as George Westinghouse and Nikola Tesla) who wanted it distributed as alternating current.

To distribute power as direct current requires a power plant every few miles. Direct current can't be transformed to a higher voltage, and transmitting it at lower voltages makes it lose so much power that it can travel only a few miles. By using alternating current, the electricity's voltage can be raised for transmission, so power plants can be greater distances away from each other. Tesla and Westinghouse won and Edison lost.

TELEPHONE SYSTEMS

Pick up your phone to place a call and you access a system with dozens of devices that are there to help you. You may see only the telephone itself, but there is a world of reliable technology that will send your voice wherever you want it to go.

One of visible pieces of telephone technology is the insulated copper wires that carry your voice. These wires are usually the lowest wires found on utility poles. You can identify them both by their position and by comparing them to electric wires (the top wires on the pole) and cable television wires (located between the telephone and electric wires).

Telephone wires are most often bundled in one large black wire and doesn't have insulators attaching it to the pole. The telephone wires stretching from pole to pole typically contain 25 or more pairs of copper wire. Each phone connection takes one pair of wires. If your house has two different telephone lines, it has two pairs of wires.

Local telephone offices, known as central offices, control the switching and distribution of phone calls. Field cables leave a central office in bundles of thousands of pairs of wires and go to the neighborhoods and area businesses. Smaller bundles of cables called distribution cables reach out to individual neighborhoods. Along the way from the central office to a house, cables may be spliced in several places. To protect the splices from weather and insects, they are encased in splice cases. The longer the telephone cables stretch from the central office, the weaker the telephone signals are. To combat this loss of energy, phone companies install repeaters—devices that amplify the signal—along the cable.

At a house or business, a ready access terminal or connector is connected to the wires. A drop wire connects the ready access terminal to a house or business. The connection between the drop wire and interior house wires is made at a protector mounted on an outside wall of the house. The protector also protects the circuit from surges so that lightning strikes or other power surges don't travel to the telephone wires inside. All the telephone wires inside connect to the protector.

House Protector

BEHAVIOR
Houses the connector that joins the telephone wires from the utility pole to the wires in your house. It also protects the connection from power surges.

HABITAT
Mounted to the outside of houses, a few feet off the ground.

HOW IT WORKS
The older-style protector has a carbon fuse; the newer style uses a gas tube fuse. A surge of electricity burns the carbon fuse, allowing a grounding wire to come in contact with the "tip" and "ring" wires (positive and negative sides of the circuit) in the drop line. The surge then goes to the ground, thus protecting anyone using the phone. When this occurs, phone service is interrupted until the fuse is replaced. The newer gas tube protector diverts surges to ground, but then returns to normal operation without the need for a service call.

Older houses have ceramic fuses in a 6-inch-long (15-cm-long) aluminum canister. If these fuses burn out, a repair technician must replace them to restore service.

UNIQUE CHARACTERISTICS
Look for a small gray box, mounted on the outside of your home, that has wires running from the box to a utility pole.

Telephone Drop Wire

BEHAVIOR
Connects the telephones in a house or business to the wires supported by utility poles.

HABITAT
You see drop wires everywhere there is aboveground telephone service. Underground service also has a connection between the *house protector* (see page 182) and the connection box on the ground, but you can't see it because it is buried.

HOW IT WORKS
Inside the drop wire is one or, more likely, two pairs of twisted copper wires. Each pair of wires provides service for one telephone line.

Telephone Riser Pipe

BEHAVIOR

Protects telephone wires coming from underground "runs" that connect to the wires on a utility pole. In neighborhoods where telephone service is provided underground and there are no utility poles, the wires typically connect to a utility pole outside the neighborhood. They rise up from underground and continue up the utility pole. A plastic riser pipe protects the bottom few feet of the wires.

HABITAT

Wherever telephone service within a neighborhood is provided to homes or offices underground and the service to the neighborhood is provided on utility poles.

HOW IT WORKS

The riser is a tube made of metal or plastic. It hides the wires at eye level, keeps them impervious to gnawing animals and curious people, and carries the wires for underground service delivery.

UNIQUE CHARACTERISTICS

If the wires running down a utility pole are enclosed in a metal pipe or conduit, they are more likely to be electrical wires, not telephone wires.

Aerial Service Terminal

BEHAVIOR
Connects the telephone wires running to your home to those inside the cable that runs from one utility pole to the next.

HABITAT
In neighborhoods with many homes or businesses, you'll find a terminal near almost every pole. The connector is attached to the telephone wire, so it doesn't hang on the pole itself, but is quite close to the pole.

HOW IT WORKS
The terminal enables telephone workers to plug wires from a house or business into slots inside the connector, making it easy to make a connection.

UNIQUE CHARACTERISTICS
In a neighborhood that has underground utilities, the telephone wires leave the connector and run down the pole through a *telephone riser pipe* (see page 184). The connection to the wires that run to each house is made inside a *telephone pedestal* (see page 77) on the ground.

Splice Box

BEHAVIOR
Protects the splices, or connections, between the many pairs of copper wire.

HABITAT
Splice boxes are strung along telephone wires at frequent intervals.

HOW IT WORKS
Cable comes on spools of various lengths; 500 feet (150 m) is most common. At the end of one spool the wires must be connected to the wires in the next spool. In a splice box the ends of cables are joined together. The corresponding wires are aligned and the bundles are squeezed together with plastic strips.

UNIQUE CHARACTERISTICS
Some splice boxes are large shiny cylinders; others are smaller black cases.

Telephones carry voices at frequencies from 350 to 3,500 hertz. Most conversations people have are in this range, so it doesn't occur to them that the range is so limited. Humans can actually hear frequencies up to 15,000 to 18,000 hertz, and well below 350 hertz—but not through the telephone.

Load Point

BEHAVIOR
Amplifies a telephone signal to offset decreases incurred as the signal travels along a telephone wire.

HABITAT
Attached to telephone wires, often in rural areas. They are spaced 3,000 feet apart along the wires if those wires extend more than three miles from the central office. In cities, the wires don't extend that far because there are so many customers that the phone company installs many central offices. For this reason, you may not see load points in cities.

HOW IT WORKS
Coils inside a load point reduce current fluctuations caused by lightning or surges in nearby electrical wires. Electricity flowing through the coils produces a magnetic field that resists changes when the electrical current changes.

Telephone conversations travel along the copper wires as electrical signals. The voltage in the wires is about 6 to 12 volts—not enough to shock anyone. However, when there is an incoming call, the telephone central office sends a 90-volt signal along the wires to ring the bell inside the phone. This 90-volt ringing signal would produce a painful shock to anyone touching the wires.

T1-Line Extender

BEHAVIOR
Boosts the signals carried on the wires of T1 lines. T1 lines are used to connect cell phone towers to central offices and to connect large computers or offices with many telephone lines. Signals on T1 lines run at high frequencies, and since high frequency signals dissipate over a short distance, they need to be amplified.

HABITAT
On utility poles, near the ground, spaced every 6,000 feet along the routes of T1 cables.

HOW IT WORKS
T1 is a system designed to carry 24 telephone calls on just two wires (instead of 24 pairs of wires). T1 technology was a major telecommunications innovation. Instead of carrying analog telephone signals, it digitizes the signals and squeezes more data onto a pair of wires.

In conversations on common telephone wires (twisted pairs of copper wire), the signal is sent in an analog format. T1 carries the signal digitally (as a series of "0s" and "1s"). Each of the 24 phone calls is digitally encoded. Each is transmitted in sequence along the wires. A new train of 24 packets of data (from the 24 conversations) is transmitted 8,000 times each second.

UNIQUE CHARACTERISTICS
When you spot a T1-line extender, check the odometer in your car. See if you see another extender 1.2 miles (2 km) farther down the road. Their large silver drums are sometimes painted white. Some T1-line extenders have fins on their sides to help get rid of excess heat.

Service Terminal for Optical Fiber Cables

BEHAVIOR
The cans (the terminals look like cans attached to utility poles) isolate one cable from the next and give workers access to the cables for maintenance.

HABITAT
On utility poles that carry optical fibers or that are near underground optical fiber runs.

HOW IT WORKS
Many cables are pressurized to keep out moisture. This pressure also allows service crews to check for damage to the cable sheathing. If something damages a cable and the gas inside escapes, pressure drops. Crews monitor the pressure so they know if there is damage.

UNIQUE CHARACTERISTICS
It is difficult to distinguish this type of can from a *T-1 line extender* (see page 188). You have to look for a plate on the can that indicates that it's under 15 PSIG (pounds of pressure per square inch). That pressure is about one-third that of the pressure in car tires. Nitrogen is often the gas used to pressurize the cables. A gauge in the can measures the pressure inside it.

6-Pair Can

BEHAVIOR
Protects the splices for cables that have six pairs of wires.

HABITAT
Mounted below the telephone wires on the side of a utility pole.

HOW IT WORKS
Inside are 12 posts, on which the wires from the house or building are connected to the wires from above, on the utility pole.

UNIQUE CHARACTERISTIC
It is a small, shiny, rectangular metal box.

CABLE TELEVISION OR BROADBAND SERVICE

Cable companies provide cable television and fast connection to the Internet. Nearly everywhere in the United States you can find their cables on utility poles. Now, cable companies are starting to supply telephone service to homes, too.

To get to your home, cable television signals are sent to the regional "head end," or office of the cable company. The signals are sent out as light waves, which are generated by lasers. The signals travel to hubs, where the optical signals are amplified with other lasers. Hubs are nondescript buildings that house the electronics equipment. Inside them, the optical signals are regenerated and distributed along fiber-optic cable to feeder service areas.

One common type of regenerator used in cable systems is the EDFA, or Erbium-Doped Fiber Amplifier. A regenerator works by capturing the existing signal in the *doping*, or coating of a cable. A laser provides the energy to recharge the signal and send it on its way downstream.

The next components in the system are *nodes*. There the light waves are converted to electrical signals that are amplified and sent along the trunk lines. If amplification is needed along a trunk line, devices called *trunk amplifiers* are inserted into the line.

The trunk lines connect to feeder lines at *bridgers* (see page 197). Feeder lines have taps on them where wires connect to homes.

ANALOG VERSUS DIGITAL SIGNALS

Analog signals vary continuously, while digital signals have individual steps. The hands that move in most wristwatches and clocks provide time in an analog form. On the other hand, digital watches show you a specific number.

A CD records music digitally. It finds the volume for many different frequencies of sound many times a second and records each level as a bump. A vinyl record records music in analog format; each change in volume or pitch is etched into the vinyl.

Splice Enclosure

BEHAVIOR
Protects a splice of optical fiber cables.

HABITAT
Along the fiber optical cable runs, between utility poles. The cables themselves support the spice enclosures.

HOW IT WORKS
Splicing optical fibers is a tricky and time-consuming task. To make it easier to splice cables, technicians often store extra cable along the cable run so they can lower the splice to the ground to work on it. This is easier than making or repairing splices while standing in the bucket of a lift truck.

UNIQUE CHARACTERISTICS
Splice enclosures are metal cans. Where you see a splice enclosure you might also see a pair of optical fiber *shoes* (see page 193). If you see the shoes, you can be certain that that extra cable is stored there.

Shoe

BEHAVIOR

Also known as a snowshoe because of its shape, this device stores optical fiber cable. Cable can be damaged if it is bent back on itself. The shoe provides a frame to wrap the cable around so it won't be damaged.

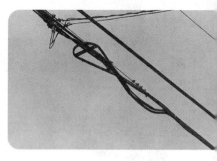

HABITAT

At nodes and splices along the routes of a cable company's optical fibers.

HOW IT WORKS

When making a splice or installing optical fibers to make a node, workers leave a few dozen extra feet of optical fiber cable. To store the cable, they loop it back down along the cable and around the outside of the shoe. The shoe supports the cable and keeps it from breaking where it bends. When workers need to service the cable, they can take it off the shoe and drop the extra length down into a truck, rather than trying to work on it perched in the air on a lift.

Tap

BEHAVIOR
Provides the connection between wires that carry cable service to a home and the distribution wires that carry the signals along the street.

HABITAT
Attached to cable television wires, close to utility poles. One tap may serve from one to several houses. In some neighborhoods you can see a tap near every utility pole or every few utility poles.

HOW IT WORKS
To connect a home to the cable system, cable company installers snap a connector into the tap. The connector leads to the wire that runs into the house.

UNIQUE CHARACTERISTICS
By looking at the taps and following the wires to homes, you can get a good idea of who in the area has cable service. However, if someone used to have cable service but has discontinued it, the wire to their house might still be there. It wouldn't, however, be connected at the tap.

If cable service is provided underground instead of from utility poles, the taps are in a metal box, called a pedestal, on the ground. Usually it is marked with the word *Television* or other words so you can distinguish it from similar-looking *telephone pedestals* (see page 77).

Line Extender

BEHAVIOR
Amplifies the signals carried by feeder cables so they can travel farther and serve more homes. Feeder cables provide television signals directly to taps.

HABITAT
Attached to the cable, near the utility pole. Line extenders are placed on cables every quarter mile (400 m) or so.

HOW IT WORKS
Line extenders amplify the radio frequency signals that travel along wires. They draw their power from power supplies that are attached to utility poles close by. Line extenders amplify the signals to a level that is high enough to provide good reception in homes. They are the last amplifiers a signal meets up with before it reaches a television set.

UNIQUE CHARACTERISTICS
They have one line coming in and one line going out. You can identify them as silver-colored boxes (they're made of aluminum) with ridges. The cables are attached to the ridges. The ridges help radiate heat so the electronics inside don't overheat.

Cable Power Supply

BEHAVIOR
Supplies electric power for the *line extenders* (see page 195). It also has a bank of three to six batteries inside in case electric power is lost.

HABITAT
Mounted directly on a utility pole. It is the large, rectangular metal box mounted on the side of the utility pole.

HOW IT WORKS
A power supply draws electricity from the electric company's wires overhead. It transforms the alternating current into the voltages needed for the cable system and converts the current into direct current. The direct current also charges the batteries stored inside the power supply.

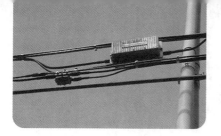

Bridger and Trunk Amplifier

BEHAVIOR
Amplifies the signal along a trunk line.

HABITAT
Bridgers and trunk amplifiers are located along the trunk cables between nodes and feeder lines. You can identify a trunk line by the absence of taps on the line. Trunk lines don't directly connect to homes. Instead, they provide signals to the feeder lines that supply homes.

Bridgers and trunk amplifiers look like large line extenders. They are difficult to differentiate from line extenders; the only visible difference is that they are on trunk lines, not feeder lines. Bridgers have one cable coming in and three going out. The three outgoing cables each serve a feeder line that may have up to three line extenders. Trunk amplifiers have one line coming in and one line going out.

HOW IT WORKS
Bridgers and trunk amplifiers work like other amplifiers (see "Line Extenders," page 195). They get their power from power supplies mounted on utility poles. They use the power to amplify the electric signals (referred to as RFs, or radio frequency signals) in the cables.

Node

BEHAVIOR

Connects optical fibers coming from hubs and metal wires that distribute the signals to homes. The node converts the signal from an optical signal to an electrical or RF (radio frequency) signal.

The television signal is carried as light waves on optical fiber from the hub to the node. The node converts it to an electrical signal and sends it out on metal wire on the trunk lines. Each node supplies up to 500 homes with cable service.

HABITAT

Some nodes are mounted on the ground inside large metal cabinets, next to utility poles to provide service underground. In locations where cable service is provided overhead, the nodes are attached to the cables up in the air, near a utility pole.

HOW IT WORKS

The signals are sent from the head end as light waves, which are generated by lasers. By shining the laser light onto a photocell, the signal is converted from light into electricity. The RF signals are fed into the lines toward consumers.

UNIQUE CHARACTERISTICS

Look for a *shoe* (see page 193) nearby. The shoe, which looks like the outline of a snowshoe, is attached to the cable overhead and is used to store extra cable near nodes.

Nodes look like large *line extenders* (see page 195). The housing that protects them is made of shiny aluminum and has ridges that help get rid of heat in the nodes.

Head End

BEHAVIOR
Generates the television signals that travel along the cable into homes.

HABITAT
Head ends are often located at the regional headquarters of each cable company.

HOW IT WORKS
The head end is the system that receives television programming in any of several formats. It picks up live and taped programs from satellite feeds via large dish antennas that are pointed toward the south. It also gets programs from videotapes or local live programs.

UNIQUE CHARACTERISTICS
You can identify the location of a head end by the presence of satellite dishes (to pick up television broadcasts from satellites) and a cable company name prominently displayed on the building.

ABOUT THE AUTHOR

Ed Sobey, PhD, operates the Northwest Invention Center in Redmond, Washington. He has previously directed several science museums and was the founding director of the National Inventors Hall of Fame and the founder of the National Toy Hall of Fame. Formerly a research scientist specializing in polar oceanography, Ed has conducted research in Antarctica and Alaska and throughout the Pacific Ocean.

Ed has written 16 books, including *Loco-Motion*, a teachers' guide to hands-on science projects, and has hosted the television show *The Idea Factory*. He also chairs the Pacific Northwest Chapter of the Explorers Club as a fellow, and runs marathons and triathlons, enjoys ocean kayaking and scuba diving.

Build potato cannons, paper match rockets, Cincinnati fire kites, tennis ball mortars, and more dynamite devices

Backyard Ballistics

Build Potato Cannons, Paper Match Rockets, Cincinnati Fire Kites, Tennis Ball Mortars, and More Dynamite Devices

BY WILLIAM GURSTELLE

A Selection of Quality Paperback Book Club

"Your inner boy will get a bang out of these 13 devices to build and shoot in your own back yard, some of them noisy enough to legally perk up a 4th of July."—THE DALLAS MORNING NEWS

"Would-be rocketeers, take note: Engineer William Gurstelle has written a book for you."—CHICAGO TRIBUNE

"William Gurstelle . . . is the Felix Grucci of potato projectiles!"
—TIME OUT NEW YORK

This step-by-step guide uses inexpensive household or hardware store materials to construct awesome ballistic devices. Features clear instructions, diagrams, and photographs that show how to build projects ranging from the simple— a match-powered rocket—to the more complex—a scale-model, table-top catapult—to the offbeat—a tennis ball cannon. With a strong emphasis on safety, the book also gives tips on troubleshooting, explains the physics behind the projects, and profiles scientists and extraordinary experimenters.

$16.95 (CAN $25.95)
ISBN-13: 978-1-55652-375-5
ISBN-10: 1-55652-375-0

Engineering the City

How Infrastructure Works
Projects and Principles for Beginners
BY MATTHYS LEVY AND RICHARD PANCHYK

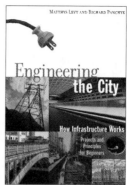

"Future engineers, math enthusiasts, and students seeking ideas for science projects will all be fascinated by this book."—BOOKLIST

How does a city obtain water, gas, and electricity? Where do these services come from? How are they transported? The answer is infrastructure, or the inner, and sometimes invisible, workings of the city. *Engineering the City* tells the fascinating story of infrastructure as it developed through history along with the growth of cities. Experiments, games, and construction diagrams show how these structures are built, how they work, and how they affect the environment of the city and the land outside it.

$14.95 (CAN $22.95)
ISBN-13: 978-1-55652-419-6
ISBN-10: 1-55652-419-6

CHICAGO REVIEW PRESS

www.chicagoreviewpress.com

Distributed by
Independent Publishers Group
www.ipgbook.com

Available at your local bookstore
or by calling (800) 888-4741